T0103686

Big Paws, Bigger Heart

A Dog's Memoir

James R. Loveless

iUniverse LLC
Bloomington

BIG PAWS, BIGGER HEART
A DOG'S MEMOIR

iUniverse books may be ordered through booksellers or by contacting:

iUniverse LLC
1663 Liberty Drive
Bloomington, IN 47403
www.iuniverse.com
1-800-Authors (1-800-288-4677)

Because of the dynamic nature of the Internet, any web addresses or links contained in this book may have changed since publication and may no longer be valid. The views expressed in this work are solely those of the author and do not necessarily reflect the views of the publisher, and the publisher hereby disclaims any responsibility for them.

Any people depicted in stock imagery provided by Thinkstock are models, and such images are being used for illustrative purposes only. Certain stock imagery © Thinkstock.

ISBN: 978-1-4917-2200-8 (sc)
ISBN: 978-1-4917-2201-5 (e)

Library of Congress Control Number: 2014901893

Printed in the United States of America.

iUniverse rev. date: 02/12/2014

To Finley and Brooks, who taught me that there is more to a dogs devotion to his best friend than ribbons and titles. My life has been greatly enriched by the lessons I learned from them. They will forever live in my heart.

Contents

Chapter 1
In the Beginning

My name is Finley, and for a dog from Colorado who had a hard time finding a home, I'd have to say the family that wound up adopting me made the wait more than worthwhile. At first, I couldn't figure out why no one wanted me; after all, I had everything going for me. I'd describe myself as having good looks, a wonderful personality, and smart-as-they-come brains with a modest persona. Maybe I'm overdoing it about the modest part, but they say it's all about how you sell yourself that makes you successful in life. Perhaps how I was perceived was the problem in finding me a home at first.

The time it took to get me adopted really wasn't that big a deal. To most people, four months would be considered a normal length of time for placing a find like me in a loving home. It wasn't the amount of time that had bothered me; it was that I was one of five boys in a litter of nine, and my huge feet made me stand out from all the rest of my siblings. This is not a redeeming quality when you're trying to get yourself placed in a good home.

All my siblings who had gone to good homes were recognized as champion quality, which left me behind, still wishing and waiting. It didn't help much that my first human dad gave me the nickname Big Paws. Despite the fact I was the cutest puppy of the bunch, people weren't looking for cute. They wanted dogs who were correct in the eyes of the American Kennel Club, and oversized feet were incorrect.

I remained behind with my birth mom and a select group of aunts, uncles, and cousins. Joni and David were my human parents, and even though they wanted to find me the perfect home, neither had any qualms about keeping me as long as I was happy, and I was. There was a nice

1

yard to run around in, and Joni started teaching me how to play on the obstacles David had built for their dog family to train and have fun on. I had my own fluffy bed to sleep in, and there was plenty of room for me. What more could a puppy want?

As I was embracing the fact that Joni and David's home in Colorado Springs was where I was going to grow up and live, I couldn't help feeling like I had another destiny. Humans drive themselves nuts trying to figure out how we know these things. Though Joni tried to reassure me this was home, somehow we both knew I was meant for another job.

On the last Saturday in April, my suspicions were finally realized. The bath tipped me off. Joni always made sure I looked my best when there was a chance I might be finding a new home. With my hair all brushed, and sporting a fancy new collar, I was dressed to the nines and ready to show that nobody could go wrong by having a dog with big paws around.

As it happened, the man and woman that showed up that Saturday afternoon were indeed interested in taking me home with them. They drove more than eighteen hundred miles, gambling that I might be the right one to replace the dog they had just lost. How I measured up to their recently departed friend would be the key to my future.

This couple happened to be from Pennsylvania, the place where David was from. The lady had a lot of experience with all kinds of dogs, but the man didn't until he had decided seven years earlier that he wanted a dog to call his own. The dog he acquired wound up becoming a very special dog who accomplished great things in his life.

The man's dog was sort of a rags-to-riches story that took him from being just another pet dog to a devoted, passionate competitor whose natural abilities allowed him to achieve things others only dream of. But where his speed, agility, and intelligence ranked him at the very top of the list of dogs that should win any contest they are entered in, it was his desire to please his owner and all who came to watch him that went far beyond winning ribbons and titles. As it turned out, it wasn't *what* he won that made him a legend; it was what he *didn't* win that made the legacy of this legendary hero.

When these folks first arrived, I wasn't aware that this legend that I speak of was this man's best friend and had just passed away. They had come all this way in the hopes of adopting me as his replacement. All I knew was that a goofy-looking guy wearing a white baseball cap with the word *Twerp* embossed on it was checking me out. He had an awestruck look on his mustached face, and he did nothing except scratch the back of his head.

I took a moment to size him up. I don't know why, but I just had the urge to jump in his arms and slime his face and glasses with kisses. I truly didn't know what this guy was all about; all I knew was that I had a strange premonition that he and I were meant for one another. After all, how could I go wrong with a guy who was so proud of who he was that he advertised it on his hat? Later, I was relieved to know he wasn't a twerp after all. His hat said *Terp*, short for Terrapin, which was the nickname of the university he supported in sports.

And so it was to be, this four-month-old big-pawed puppy with the good looks, wonderful personality, brains, and modest persona was to become the heir to the kingdom of a legend that so many loved to watch perform. In becoming his beneficiary, I had to first learn the lessons he learned in order to follow in his footsteps and become my own legend. Though he wasn't around to teach them to me, everything he did was etched in the minds of those who had experienced his wonderful life, and that became the foundation of what my life was to be.

Chapter 2
His Name Was Brooks

Brooks was a Belgian Tervuren who started out his life competing in beauty contests. People call it breed competition or conformation, but us canines look at it as getting extra rewards for being handsome and pretty. A woman in suburban Maryland adopted him when he was three months old, solely for his looks. He won blue ribbons for Jean in the breed ring, the only thing that mattered in her world of show dogs.

What Jean told the breeder to obtain him is anybody's guess, but whatever it was it worked, since he was the pick of his litter. Usually for someone to get a dog of his caliber, one would have to assure the breeder that only the best would be provided for the dog, and having about a grand in cash also helped. When his new mom got him, Brooks was named Jashes Atticus of Ubar. Good god! Who names a dog Jashes? Sounds like a name for some Greek godlike figure made of stone, not a fun-loving puppy. To me, his name was Brooks.

He grew up with three brothers and a sister. They all were basenjis, and none of them were like him. They were cute and fun, but they were only brothers and sister because they shared the same house; other than that, they had little or no contact with one another.

Sadly, as Brooks grew up, he spent most of his time in a crate. In the morning, he was let out to eat and get a little exercise, but he never got to play with the basenjis. Crated all day with little to do but sleep, he was again let out in the evening to eat and get some playtime. He went back in the crate at night and repeated the ritual the next day. This was his life every day.

When he got a little older, he went to classes to learn how to act in the ring for the shows he was going to be entered in. In class, he was a

4

natural at all the moves and rituals that he had to go through. That was where Brooks learned to get the most out of what little life he had. He figured that if he could be the best dog ever at this beauty contest thing he was being forced into doing, maybe he'd get a chance to do something else. He wanted anything but that life, and he knew it wasn't the life he was destined for. Brooks wanted to run, play, catch, and eat as he saw humans do on the television.

From where his crate was set up in the corner of Jean's living room, he had an excellent view of the twenty-seven-inch Sony Trinitron in front of the room. He learned a lot from that TV; it was the only thing that made life tolerable in his crate. Brooks's take on life was that humans and dogs had a lot in common. Both liked to run, play catch, and eat. These were three of his favorite things, but he had few chances to do them.

Over the next couple of months, he became a big guy, sturdy and strong. He had a beautiful, shiny fawn and mahogany coat and a long silky tail that waved over his body like a sail in the wind when he pranced. He smiled with the confidence of a winner, knowing all he had to do was strike his stand. No one could come close to beating him.

When the time came to enter the ring, he simply blew the competition away. In every show he entered, he took first place. His confidence grew along with his physical size. He grew so fast that his crate got too small for him, but little did anyone know that this would affect his destiny. Growing up in an undersized crate simply wasn't working. When he grew to more than twice the size of his brothers and sister, it was too much to handle for his owner. Life for Jashes Atticus of Ubar went from bad to worse.

The life of a Belgian Tervuren puppy should be full of fun things, such as playing with friends, enjoying toys, getting dirty in the yard, and having lots to eat. Nothing could be further from that life than what Brooks was enduring. He never got to play with the basenjis or other friends. The only friends he had were competitors in the ring, and they all despised him for denying them the chance to experience the winners' circle. His lone toy was a rope with a knot in the middle; the basenjis had stuffed hedgehogs and tennis balls to chase.

Brooks once snagged a fleece bear that was left behind by one of his brothers when he was being led into his crate for the night. He loved sleeping with it. Snuggling up with that thing made his night. The next morning, when Jean let Brooks outside for his duty call, she discovered him carrying it with him to the yard.

Jerking it angrily from his mouth, she scolded him harshly, "Bad dog. Bad, bad dog. These aren't your toys."

She took the bear away, and he never enjoyed it again. From that day on, he tore up every stuffed toy he ever had. Lord forbid that he track mud in the house because his life would become a living hell. Eating was limited to keep his girlish figure in check for the judges. He was passionate about food and loved anything that had flavor or smell, but this was denied, since it was all about the breed ring.

When Brooks was thirteen months old, something started to happen that changed his life forever. In every show Jean attended with Brooks, he wound up with no other entries. If there were no other entries, Brooks couldn't get the points he needed to be crowned a champion, which was Jean's ultimate goal. The word was out. If Jashes Atticus of Ubar was entered in a show, the competition stayed away. The fix was in, and there wasn't a single thing Jean could do about it. Brooks was simply too good to show.

Once in a great, great while, a dog comes around who is too good to show, and that's just what Brooks had become.

Chapter 3
A Whole New World

As fate would have it, a woman in Pennsylvania happened to be looking for a Tervuren or Terv, as we are commonly referred to. Her husband wanted to adopt a dog so they could share a common interest. When they lived in Maryland, she became hooked on Tervs when she learned firsthand that the two chow chows she had been raising weren't exactly what she had bargained for. They turned out to be very independent and proved to be quite a handful. They were very loyal and loving, but when it came to doing obedience work, they could be as stubborn as a groom saying yes at the altar.

One of the chows was a big, handsome blond boy named Shemp. Once on a walk, a little girl mistook him for a lion, a mystique he carried from that day on. Pandora was much smaller and had a striking resemblance to a small black bear cub and the rowdiness to boot.

It was fun having a lion and a bear for pets; at least that's what the chow experience became for the couple. Having observed the border collies at Shemp's obedience classes, they marveled over their amazing attention and agility. That's what the couple was really looking for, but they knew full well that border collies weren't the answer for a couple living in a suburban townhouse. They were just too tightly wound and wouldn't be practical. Can you imagine a border collie with two chows in a townhouse? Now that would be an adventure I'd like to hear about. But the more they observed, the greater their desire became to find a breed that could manage in such an environment while still having the traits of a border collie.

One night after poring over numerous breed magazines, the description of the Belgian Tervuren caught the woman's eye: *Intelligent,*

7

courageous, and alert, marked by its devotion to work and family. Elegant in appearance, the Belgian Tervuren's color is a rich fawn to russet mahogany with black overlay. The Terv excels in obedience and agility competitions; this breed also makes an excellent therapy or guide dog for the disabled, as well as being outstanding at their original job of herding. An intelligent, sensitive dog, the Belgian Tervuren makes a wonderful addition to any home.

"That's it," she proclaimed. "That's the breed we've been looking for." The search to find the right Belgian Tervuren was on, and the woman would leave no stone unturned in her quest.

In her search, she met numerous breeders and got quite an education on what Tervs were all about, but few were available at an affordable price. For such a rare breed, it was amazing how many people owned Tervs, but if you weren't a member of their good-old-boy network, no one was willing to help you out.

One breeder did come forward to help. Marian had numerous Tervuren, all of breed quality and every one a champion. There was a huge waiting list for her puppies when her girls had litters, and all were claimed well before they hit the ground. Not only that, they were very expensive and way out of reach for what the couple could afford.

For some reason, Marian took a liking to the woman and helped her find a breeder who just happened to have a little three-month-old Terv puppy. Less than breed quality, this little girl was love at first sight; with that, the match was made. Vanah became the perfect fit for those two chows, and they quickly became attached as if she were a chow herself. Vanah fit in so well that she strangely developed a dark purple spot on her tongue that was reminiscent of the purple tongues of her adopted brother and sister. It was said that it was the chow in her.

The next year was a happy time for the family; however, times change and the husband's work forced them to move to Pennsylvania. At the same time, Shemp developed very bad hips and they lost him late in their first winter up north. Vanah also developed some health problems of her own, which contributed to her slow growth. At almost two years of age, she resembled a Terv, but she was a third smaller than the norm. Her condition was attributed to a bad thyroid that caused her to have little to no appetite. With no aspirations of showing her in breed, her obedience career was very much up in the air. She had no energy to concentrate or perform. After she was put on the proper medication, her appetite came back, and she started to become the Terv she was meant to be.

The damage was done though. She would never grow up to become the normal size of a Tervuren.

Marian stayed in touch with Vanah's owner. She knew the health problems that she was having with Vanah and felt somewhat responsible even though she had only recommended Vanah's breeder. But that was the way Marian was, and that was why her pups were in such high demand. She cared for both the dogs and the owners that she put with them, and she always tried to make things right.

Marian had bred Brooks, and she was all too aware of his situation with Jean. She knew that the woman in Maryland would never give up on Vanah, and she heard that the husband was interested in finding a Tervuren for himself. It seemed too good to be true, a natural fit. She could satisfy her guilt about Vanah and find a good proven home for Brookie. The negotiations began soon.

Brooks was sold to the folks in Pennsylvania for five hundred dollars, and they would get legal custody. They had to finish his title to make him champion, and if he were to be bred, Jean would get half of the sire fee for every time he got it on, so to speak. I'm guessing that's a bonus old Brookie never expected.

The deal was inked on March 10, 1993, and Jashes Atticus of Ubar was renamed Brooks Robinson of Loveless. Unfortunately, the American Kennel Club knew him only by his original name, which Dad later tried to change, but to no avail. It didn't matter because Brooks was reborn, and the only thing left to do was to introduce him to his new family.

Chapter 4
The Legend Begins

When the day came for Brooks to meet his new folks, he was unaware of what was going on. He knew things were not quite right when he noticed Jean gathering up all his things after his usual morning routine. He did not have that many to start with, and she put them in a brown grocery bag.

When he went to shows, only his leashes and liver treats would go with him, and he knew something was up. As she tidied up the room, he thought, *Visitors?*

He never recalled visitors coming to see him. Something was going on, and it involved him. He was very anxious to find out what. Whenever Brooks suspected change, his adrenaline would take over. He'd also get very hyper. Tervs often get upset by change. It's a trait we all seem to have. I can't explain it; it just is what it is. There wasn't much he could do in his small crate, but he whimpered and pawed at the crate door to get some attention. It was a waste of energy; Jean just went to another room, leaving Brooks to wait and wonder.

An hour passed, and Brooks settled down. He thought nothing would come of the earlier events, but the doorbell rang.

Ding dong. Ding dong!

All hell broke loose when Brooks jumped up in his crate, sending it two feet into the end table. A crashing sound echoed throughout the house.

Ruff, ruff, ruff.

Bang, bang, bang.

Ruff, ruff.

Bang!

The racket made Operation Rolling Thunder sound like a Girl Scout picnic.

From the other side of the door, a man said, "Holy crap! What the heck is that?"

From the kitchen, Jean tore into the living room. "Coming! Don't mind the puppy!"

The man said, "Puppy? Sounds more like they have a grizzly in there. Good god. You sure we have the right house?"

Brooks had never seen Jean scramble so fast. She looked like a quarterback fleeing a pursuing linebacker. He thought he saw her leap over the coffee table to get the dislodged crate that was making such a racket.

"I'll be there in a second. Just hang in there," she yelled, trying to sound calm.

Under her breath, but loud enough for Brooks to hear, she said, "Mind your manners. Those are your new owners. Behave, big guy. Behave now!"

New owners? Could that be true? Did I hear right? New owners? Trying to control his emotions, Brooks quelled his bark to a loud squealing whimper. He stepped up his running in place, which made more racket in that crate than his barking did.

Jean tried her hardest to calm Brookie down without losing her temper in front of the prospective owners. "Jashes, quiet, boy."

A female voice on the other side of the door whispered, "I wonder what's going on in there? I'm starting to have second thoughts."

"Jashes?" the man said. "We're spending five hundred bucks for a Jashes?"

Jean opened the door and said, "Hi. You must be Mr. and Mrs. Loveless?" She pulled herself together and stood at attention after straightening her blouse. Running her fingers through her hair and out of her eyes, she presented her hand to the man.

"Yeah. I'm Jim, and this is my wife, Leslie," he said quietly.

"We're here about adopting your Terv," Leslie said as she stood outside on the stoop, trying to see what had caused all the commotion.

"Yes, yes, yes. Come right in, please. I'm Jean." She led them through the foyer and into the living room. "We talked briefly on the phone. I believe Marian finalized everything with you, and all that is left to be done is to see if Jashes is a good fit for your family."

11

Jim looked at Leslie and said, "Jashes?"

"Yes, that's right. Jashes Atticus of Ubar. That's his name," Jean chimed in proudly. "He's a wonderful boy and quite good in the ring. I'm thrilled he's going to a home where he can have more opportunities than I could provide." Jean really cared for him deep down. He was an experiment that didn't work out, and she only wanted the best for him.

Brooks had heard right. *These folks must be my new family.*

While standing in the area that led to the living room, Leslie and Jim were in clear view for Brooks to size up. Leslie wasn't very tall, and she was slight with short blonde hair and a light complexion. She had a soft touch and a quiet demeanor that melted away the tough-guy attitude Brooks had with strangers.

He thought Jim was goofy. He was of medium height and build and had a dark complexion. *What's with this look? He looks like Weird Al Yankovic in a Phillies hat! Is that what a dad's supposed to look like? Jury's out on this dude, but he talks a good game. I'll cut him some slack for now.*

As they approached his crate, Brooks let out a series of barks that shook the house. His tail was banging the crate. His sudden eruption even took Jean off guard.

"Quiet, boy. Settle down. Settle down," she pleaded. "You misbehave, and these nice folks will go home without you."

When Brooks carried on even louder, Jean was at a loss. If she let him out while he was acting like this, lord knows what might happen. Someone might get hurt.

"If you don't mind, can I jump in here?" Leslie made her way over to the crate. "I have some experience with this kind of situation. We have chow chows at home, and they are famous for acting like this."

Jean stepped aside and said, "Be my guest."

Leslie calmly approached the crate, kneeling in front of the door and petting the ground. "Quiet, boy. Easy does it. You're a handsome man, aren't you?" She put her hand against the door and let him sense that she meant him no harm.

He suddenly stopped barking and slowly put his head forward to smell her palm, which was pressed flat against the wire slats.

"What a good boy," she praised him over and over in a soft tone. "You're going to be fine. Just chill out for a few moments."

Jean said, "I never saw him like this, and you got him calmed down. Wow. I'm impressed."

Hanging back and standing proud with his arms crossed, Jim said, "It was nothing. You just have to know what you're doing. That's all."

Leslie turned and cut him a stare that would mow down a five-acre cornfield.

He added, "And she sure knows what she's doing. Good job, honey." He faded back to watch her work more of her magic.

Turning her attention back to Brookie, she continued to let him sniff her hand and let him start kissing her through the wire door. "That's all you need. Just a little time to get acquainted. Now let's see how you'll be when I open the door." Moving back from in front of the crate, Leslie allowed enough room to slowly swing open the door.

Brooks pushed back into the crate, not sure about what was coming next.

With the door wide open, they faced one another. Leslie sat in front of the open crate, and Brooks backed into the rear of the enclosure.

Hoping that they might be bringing home a new addition to their family, she had put a baggie of cut-up hot dog in her coat pocket. She took out a piece, put it in the palm he had been kissing through the crate, and held it out to him.

Brooks leaned forward, slowly sniffed, and took the treat. He retreated to his original position.

"What a good boy. Want another?" She repeated the procedure several times, slowly stood up, took a couple of steps back from the open door, and motioned for him to come out.

Brooks didn't know what to make of this. Though he had gone in and out of the crate zillions of times for Jean, this was a different situation. She wasn't demanding, "Come now." She was like a lot of people on the TV. Why was he having such a hard time meeting them?

You're blowing this, dummy. Don't screw this up. They seem like nice people—even though that guy needs a haircut. Well, here goes.

Brooks emerged slowly from his crate and stood square in front of Leslie.

She bent down so he could give her a kiss, and he planted one square on her cheek. But much to their surprise, he turned and suddenly bolted past Leslie. He leaped four feet in the air into Jim's chest, knocking him back into a stuffed chair. If a guy could drown from kisses, it would have been him. Jim tried to kiss Brooks too. It was a sight to behold. Even Jean couldn't keep from laughing her big ass off. To this day, it's a mystery what happened that March morning that caused the immediate bond that lasted the rest of Brooks's life. That reaction would repeat itself seven years later.

The good-byes were short and sweet.

Brooks had proven to be a little more to handle than the basenjis were for Jean, but there were good times to remember too. After all, he had won blue ribbons for her in every show she had entered him in. She insisted on bringing him out to the truck, kind of a farewell walk.

He pranced as beautifully as ever, just like he was showing in the ring.

When they got to the vehicle, she bent down and gave him a big hug good-bye and handed the lead to Jim. She said, "He's yours now. Take good care of him." She turned and walked away without looking back.

Jim opened the door of the Ford Bronco, and Brooks leaped inside as if he'd been doing it forever.

Looking back to see if Jean would give a final wave good-bye, they saw the vacant front stoop. The house looked cold and dark.

"I guess we should have expected that," Jim muttered, pulling out into the street.

Chapter 5
Home at Last

The drive to Blooming Glen, Pennsylvania, took about three and a half hours, taking into account a few rest stops. Everything went a-okay according to Brooks, and as they approached the sleepy little town, he sat back and took everything in as best as a thirteen-month-old Belgian Tervuren puppy from Bethesda, Maryland, could.

Blooming Glen was a quiet little village about thirty-five miles north of Philadelphia. Less than five hundred people resided there, and for the most part, the folks minded their own business. There were the usual busybodies who had to be the first to know what was going on, but for the most part, it was a great place to live. There was a post office in the center of the town, an antique shop or three, Blooming Glen Pork (where everyone bought their bacon), and Moyer's Auto. Moyer's Auto was right next door to Jim and Leslie's house, and it was the focal point of the town.

Everybody took their cars, trucks, and tractors to Harley for repair. Harley Moyer owned and ran the place, and no nicer guy existed. He was born and raised in Blooming Glen, dating back to the beginning of time, it seemed. Jim always said he reminded him of the character Uncle Joe in *Petticoat Junction*. Far from being the lazy loafer that Uncle Joe was in the TV series, they looked a lot alike, and their mannerisms were similar.

Harley knew everything about the town and everybody in it. A number of the old-timers hung out in front of his shop when the weather permitted, and their gossip spread like wildfire. Harley always made it a point to listen but never tell. If you wanted the truth, he was the one to talk to, but he wouldn't gossip. Harley liked Jim and kept him informed about everything going on around town that he thought

15

would affect him. Whenever Jim was mowing the yard or puttering around with his truck, Harley would come over to say hello and fill him in on what was up.

The morning before Jim left to get his new boy, Harley had come over and asked about the new dog he was getting. Jim was amazed that anyone knew of their venture since he and Leslie had told no one about the trip. The only ones who were aware of the news were Vanah and Pandora. Who would they tell? Clyde? Harley's Aussie mix had the run of the neighborhood.

When they pulled up in the driveway at 113 Main Street, Dad about ran the truck into the door of the garage because Clyde was standing in the parking lot like he was the host of *Entertainment Tonight*. Behind him, the usual group of gabmasters waited to gossip for all to hear that wanted to hear.

When Jim parked the Bronco in front of the house, he let out a big sigh and said, "We're home, big guy."

Brooks was rigid as he peered out the rear window to take in all that was around him. So far, he liked what he had seen. The small brick-and-stone two-story Cape Cod sat on a knoll on the front quarter of a totally fenced acre-and-a-half yard. It was just prime for a dog.

While Jim fastened the lead to his collar, Leslie hurried in the front door. This bought a little time for the girls to be let outside to do their business. They'd been cooped up since early morning and were at their limit before their bladders would give out. It also gave them time to get Brooks in the house without a riot breaking out. Brooks wasn't aware that he was to be a brother to two sisters. The girls had heard Mom and Dad talking about adopting a brother for them, but it hadn't really sunk in. Life in the south end of Blooming Glen was about to change forever.

Chapter 6
Brooks Meets His New Sisters

Before Jim entered the house, he took a strong hold on the lead. He knew it would take every ounce of strength to keep the great Terv from dragging him up the stoop and through the glass storm door. Also the distance from the entrance of the house and the busy road that ran in front was a mere fifty feet. The last thing he wanted was for his new boy to tangle with the traffic that was whizzing by.

Once they were out of the truck, all bets were off. It was a scene right out of the closing credits of *The Jetsons*. Brooks took off like a shot, taking Jim's arm with him. Thank god that it stayed attached. He headed straight for the front door and stopped a foot shy of crashing through it.

Jim wasn't as lucky, winding up over the rail but managing to hang on to the tough leather lead. He recalled later that Brooks was the only dog he knew who could stop on a dime and give nine cents' change.

After letting the girls out into the yard to get some exercise, Leslie came to the front door and noticed Brooks sitting there all alone. When she saw Jim on his knees on the other side of the rail, she snapped, "You can do the weeding later. We need to get your boy settled. Quit clowning around."

Jim was the Rodney Dangerfield of the family, getting no respect.

Upon entering the house, Jim sat Brooks down for a moment and took in the reality that he now had a dog he could call his own. Kneeling down, he said, "I want you to know me as Dad and Leslie as Mom. The past is gone, and your future is now with us. Get used to being loved like you should be."

Brooks looked at his new dad like he understood and proceeded to give him another kiss. It was a moment they never forgot.

17

While Brooks was getting the nickel tour of his new home, Vanah and Pandora returned to the back door. Usually their parents were there to let them in—but not on this occasion.

"You think they are ever going to let us in?" Vanah said.

Five, ten, fifteen minutes ticked by without a sign of anyone at the door.

"I'm hungry," Dory snarled. "Let us in!"

In the hope of getting some attention, they started barking and scratching at the door.

When Brooks showed up, time froze. It seemed like an eternity for the girls to size Brooks up and for him to figure them out. In seconds, all hell broke loose. The eruption that came from the back of that house that evening was epic. Only separated by a storm door, Vanah started lunging and banging on the glass and barking her head off. "Who are you and what are you doing in my house?"

Taking the defensive, Brooks started barking and sprung back into the kitchen table. He knocked over two chairs, and the silverware and plates crashed to the floor.

Startled by the noise, Van retreated, bowling over several flowerpots and some garden tools on the deck. A metal garbage can boomed down the hill.

Gaining composure, both dogs roared back and shouted dog obscenities at one another. Only the thin glass that separated them kept from tearing each other apart. Their yowls and roars echoed through the town like a locomotive, stirring up every canine for miles around.

Mom and Dad had gone out to the truck to bring in the rest of his things when the hostilities began. Dad had his hands full of bags, but he heard the commotion and scrambled up the front stoop in a blaze. He overshot his landing zone and went over the rail again.

His accidents at the front entrance became such a ritual that the neighbors started scoring his landing on a one-to-ten point system. I think they gave him an eight on that one.

Mom sprinted past our fallen hero, flung open the front door, and charged into the battle zone. She yelled, "Cease and desist!"

There was silence. Bewildered, both dogs stood back from the war zone and anxiously waited to see what would come next.

A few moments later, Dad staggered in with an empty bag in his hand. Its contents were strewn from the front porch to the kitchen. Half out of breath, he yelled, "Cease and desist!"

Brooks looked at his new dad and tilted his head. *Is he for real?*

It took everything for Mom to keep from breaking out in total laughter. She said, "You have a twig in your hair."

As usual, he was late for the party.

Wasting no time, Dad got hold of Brooks's collar, snapped on a leash, and calmly led him into the living room to wait for Mom to deal with the girls. Brooks was shivering with excitement in the anticipation that he was going to meet this skinny little bitch who was giving him such an earful. *She may have been here first, but I'm here now. I'm ready to take charge. Besides, I'm cool. I rode in a Bronco!*

Outside, Vanah was pacing all over and whimpering as she always did when she got excited. "Who's this brute think he is, taking over my house like this? Let me in there, and I'll fix his ass," she muttered as she stomped back and forth past the door.

When Mom came out to calm Van down, it only made her more furious to see that she had a leash in her hand. "What's that for? Why do I have to wear that? He's the one that started all this." She darted from side to side, making it very difficult for her mom to fasten the lead to her collar. She showed her displeasure with every move.

"Stop it right now!" Mom commanded. "You don't see your new brother acting like this, do you?" As she finally got control of her young Terv, she got the lead fastened and gently pulled her aside. "Now we're going inside. You are going to meet your new brother, and you are going to behave." Gently stroking the fine fur that graced Vanah's neck, she looked in her dark brown eyes and said, "We are going to make this work. You can do it the easy way or the hard way. Either way, you are going to get along."

Van said, "Why not let me do it the Terv way? I'll herd his big fat ass out the front door so he can go back to where he came from." After a few minutes went by, she changed her mind. "It might not be that bad. After all, I was here first. Even that dumb lug has to know that bitches rule! I am woman, and he certainly heard me roar." Vanah positioned herself in front of the door to show she was willing to cooperate, gave a couple of shakes to straighten her hair, and gave a motion to indicate that she was ready.

19

In the living room, Dad had smartly turned on the TV for Brooks in an attempt to divert his attention from what was going on outside, and it seemed to be working. In fact, it was working too well. Father and son focused on an old episode of *The Andy Griffith Show*.

Brooks was marveling at the resemblance that Barney Fife had to his new dad. I had that same thought at times. As they fixated on the screen, Mom quietly made her way into the room, tightly grasping Vanah's short lead.

"Isn't that cute?" Mom said. "Two boobs and a tube."

Both boys turned from what they were watching and quickly raised to their feet. Dad held tight to the lead.

Brooks started forward, trembling with excitement, but Dad backed him down to a sit. Looking up at Dad, he pleaded, "Let me go. I won't do anything bad. I just want to sniff her a little."

Vanah remained unusually calm, which made Mom hold on all the tighter.

"Do I trust her?" she asked.

"I'll hold him," Dad said. "Let her have some slack on the lead. Let's see what they do."

Vanah felt the pressure release from her leash and quickly took advantage, jumping forward to sniff Brooks's neck.

The big Terv quickly twisted forward so they were both sniffing each other, and they seemed to like each other's scents.

Resisting any harsh or sudden restraint, Mom and Dad released their leashes to allow the dogs to further investigate each other. I know canines have superior smelling equipment to humans, and we can tell a lot by sniffing, but who started the tradition of sniffing butts? I quite frankly find it repulsive, but who am I judge. Let the ass sniffing begin.

I heard Ole Brooks was quite the ladies' man, and even though Vanah was now his sister, he knew a sexy bitch when he saw one. After all, he was a brother from a different mother. As their parents backed off to allow the two more freedom, they found they could bury the hatchet over the earlier incident at the back door and get along.

Vanah shot into the kitchen and playfully flopped down on the floor.

Brooks looked up at Dad for approval.

When Jim nodded, they scurried back and forth between the living room and the kitchen.

Standing aside to allow the two to play, the relieved parents congratulated each other on how well they had handled things.

"Masterfully done," Mom proclaimed.

"We couldn't ask for better."

As they watched the two dogs roll on the floor like best friends, Mom suddenly came down with a horrified look on her face. "Good god!" She ran out to the kitchen and said, "Where's Pandora?"

"Oh crap," Dad exclaimed. "We forgot all about Dory!"

They rushed to the back door and looked outside.

Brooks and Vanah followed closely behind, not wanting to miss out on anything. Stopping short of the door slamming shut in their faces, they looked at one another.

"Do we do everything in fast motion around here?" Brooks asked.

"Get used to it, bro. You're a Loveless now," Vanah proclaimed.

As Mom stayed up on the deck, Dad ran out to the yard to look for the forgotten chow. A trail of garbage led him to the trashcan that had been on the deck prior to the earlier skirmish. It was now down in the middle of the yard. He also saw a hairy black butt and a furry tail protruding from it.

"I found Dory!" Dad yelled. "Everything's fine!" He grabbed the little dog and pulled her out of the can.

In her mouth, she had the tin foil pan of the Stouffer's lasagna from dinner the night before. It was just about licked clean.

"I'm sorry, sweetie, I didn't mean to leave you out here all alone," Dad said. "Let's go up and see your new brother."

As she reluctantly made her way up to the house, Dad kept apologizing and asking her to forgive him.

She grumbled, "Shove your apologies. I was hungry. The introductions can wait."

Chapter 7
Settling In

While Dad was battling it out with the AKC over his son's name, Brooks was enjoying his new home and settling in just fine. Both sisters seemed to like their new brother. Vanah loved having another Terv to play with. Having grown up with the chows, she found they weren't quite as playful as her new brother turned out to be.

When the weather started to get nice, Brooks and Vanah loved to go outside to tear around the yard and play what Dad called "Terv Tag." It would usually start out with both dogs making a beeline to the center of the backyard. One of them, usually Brooks, would sit on a knoll while watching the other take off and circle around the entire perimeter of the area two or three times with increased velocity on every pass. The final run would just nip past the other's nose so as to provoke a high-speed run rivaling Steve McQueen's famous *Bullitt* chase scene in the movies.

Tapping their endless herding energies, they would fly around the yard, darting from left to right in an attempt to fake the other out to gain as much advantage as they could and leave the other in the dust. Brooks was a little bit faster, but Van more than compensated for her lack of speed with her tremendous agility and quickness. When Brookie was just about to catch his sister, she had the ability to make a hard cut one way or the other, causing the faster dog to overshoot and allow her to speed away.

When Vanah was pursuing Brooks, he had to take a different tactic. As Van would bear down on her brother, he didn't have the ability to make the hard cuts at high speed; instead, he simply rolled to one side or the other, causing her to have to jump over the downed Terv. Once she overshot her prey, Brooks simply rolled back up and raced the other way. This would go on seemingly forever, and there was never a clear winner,

22

just two very exhausted Tervurens flopping down in the shade of a walnut tree to get their breath before doing it all over again.

Mom and Dad could never get enough of watching them from the deck and marveling at their awesome abilities. Dad wished the Philadelphia Eagles had a couple of running backs with his Terv's abilities. At Moyer's Auto Care, Harley would kid that his business picked up on account of the show the Tervs put on. He joked about advertising entertainment during oil changes.

Life was good with Brooks in the family. The girls got along fine with him; even though there were some minor territorial squabbles that had to be settled, nothing amounted to much. There was plenty of room for everyone. They had their own oversized crates, but none of them were forced to reside in them. Unlike the first thirteen months of his life, the doors always remained open so they could come and go as they pleased. Each had a bed, water tray, and toys, so they did not mind staying in them when they were made to do so. Mandatory crate time was restricted mainly to when Mom and Dad went out, leaving no humans to supervise. Also if they were being punished, they were asked to stay in confinement for a while to reflect on their misdeeds. Sometimes I don't mind being sent to my crate when I do something wrong.

They all had their own sleeping places. Pandora liked the seclusion of the den, although occasionally, she would sleep in her crate when she wanted to feel secure. She liked it cool, and the den on the far side of the house was perfect for her.

Vanah chose Mom and Dad's bed, and she snuggled between them. It was comfortable and secure, and that's what it was all about for her. Brooks at first slept in his crate out of force of habit, since it was the only place he knew to sleep. He also liked the nice, fluffy bed and the room to stretch out without bumping into anyone. That was his place of rest until one night a couple of weeks after he arrived when he couldn't get to sleep. Not knowing whether it was because he had settled down too early or had not gotten enough exercise that day, he became restless.

At one o'clock in the morning, after everyone had gone to bed, he started roaming throughout the dark house. He ended up in the master bedroom. Mom and Dad were fast asleep, and Vanah was curled up at Dad's feet, dead to the world. Without arousing anyone, he somehow managed to jump onto the bed and stretch out in the middle, resting his head on the edge of Dad's pillow. He dozed off to dreamland, no one the wiser.

When morning arrived, Dad rolled over, unaware that he was face-to-face with the slumbering dog. He was suddenly awakened by a wet, slobbering snort. Brooks gave him a long, slimy good-morning lick from his chin straight up to his forehead. It was a scene straight out of the comic strip *Marmaduke.*

"Good god," he groaned, stirring Mom and Vanah from their snoozes. "You've got to be kidding me."

Awake now, all eyes were on Brooks. He was stretched out on his side between Mom and Dad. He tried to act innocent, as if he belonged there, but the thumping of his tail gave him away. He couldn't keep a straight face.

"Brooks!" Mom proclaimed, trying to keep a straight face herself. "So this is how it's going to be, huh?"

Brooks proceeded to kiss her face until she relented. "It's okay, boy. It's okay!"

Dad leaned over and pulled the ever-happy Terv over to him, hugging him. He whispered, "I hope your sister doesn't mind you being up here."

Van sighed and said, "Paybacks are hell, you big oaf. Wait till I get you out in the yard playing tag. Your ass will be mine." She fell back asleep.

Chapter 8
Show and Go

It took about a month to strike a new standard of normalcy. On weekdays, Dad was off to work early, and everyone else slept in until Mom got up at around seven. They all went out before breakfast to take care of their business and then ate and relaxed until Mom let them out for morning playtime around ten or so.

When the weather was good, they'd stay out until afternoon and then come in for naptime. Before their dinner, which was around five, they'd go out again for about a half an hour. Prior to Dad coming home, the evening playtime would commence and continue until after he ate. If Dad didn't have any chores, everybody got his full attention by refereeing a game of tag or playing catch with a tennis ball or Frisbee. They were out of luck if the Phillies, Orioles, or any of his other sports teams were playing on TV. Dad hated to miss out on any of their games.

Everything outside of work seemed to revolve around Dad's wide world of sports, from bumper stickers supporting the Eagles and Phillies to jerseys and hats for all his teams. It was only fitting that his dog be named after a hero from his baseball world.

Dad was not the breed show type. He was more into competitions that were judged on brawn and physical ability instead of looks and class. He managed to get through Mom's attempts at exposing him to the finer side of dog shows. He even attended a local show, but having grown up in the stick-and-ball world of sports, it wasn't his thing—and he didn't look good in plaid pants.

Their dilemmas were how were they going to show Brooks and who was going to handle him. The *how* part wasn't that big a problem—they could simply find some shows and enter him—but the *who* part was a major quandary. Dad suggested that Mom do it. Mom suggested that he go to blazes. Though she was open minded about breed competition and understood the purpose of proper breeding standards, the politics that surrounded the events weren't for her.

The Hilltown Dog Training Club was the obvious answer. It was where Mom took Vanah for obedience training. Though Hilltown had no formal breed-handling classes, many of its members showed their dogs in breed and knew a lot about it. She would find the answers to their questions at the club.

Tuesday nights were obedience nights. Up until Dad got Brooks, he rarely went to the club. The classes were held at a volunteer firehouse, and guys rarely attended. When Dad showed up, he was always asked to roll the rubber mats onto the concrete floor of the hall. Helping set up wasn't so bad, but hanging around for two hours and having to clean and roll the mats back up was enough to make him stay away.

He got a kick out of the rare occasions when the huge siren on the roof went off. He had never heard such a racket. It was hard to tell which was louder: the siren or all the dogs howling. It was worth the trip to watch everyone scramble to control the dogs and try to gain control of the chaos, but it didn't happen very often.

Dad went to the Tuesday class for two reasons, but neither was to listen for the siren. The first and foremost reason was to enroll Brooks and Dad in beginner's obedience class. The second reason was so that Mom could ask around about breed handlers.

It turned out to be a very worthwhile adventure. Dad and Brooks got to meet their new instructor who outlined all the things they were going to learn in the coming weeks. Most importantly to Dad, there was no formal dress code. If he were to elect to go into obedience competition, he could continue to wear his Phillies cap. Though the routine for a novice in obedience training seemed a bit on the dull side, there was logic to it. The sit, stay, heel, and come exercises built a foundation to the fun stuff ahead. Dad couldn't wait to get started.

Mom also found it very informative, since just about all the folks in the club had experience with breed competitions. A funny coincidence happened with the two ladies who wanted to help out the most. They both had the same first name as Mom. As Mom got more involved in the organization, the three became good friends, and the club became famous for its Leslies.

26

One evening, Mom got the name of a husband-and-wife team who she thought would be perfect for handling Brooks. It was a good night all around, and to top it all off, the siren went off, sending Brooks off into the night to a rousing choir of howls. Life was good.

Several days went by before Mom was able to get ahold of the couple. When she finally contacted them, they were more than willing to help them out. Sharon and Don had a ton of experience at handling dogs in all levels of competition. Sharon was an expert at handling dogs in the breed ring, and Don specialized more in the three levels of obedience competition. Sharon seemed willing to work with them, but she wanted to see Brooks firsthand before they committed to anything.

The only opportunity for this was the Tuesday night when Dad and Brooks were to attend their first beginner's obedience class. With three shows coming up in the next month, that was Sharon's only available night. Mom had scheduled a trip to Maryland to visit her mother and was concerned about letting Dad loose with Brooks on his own. She made it a point to let everyone know that Dad would be traveling alone with a dog in his truck for the first time. She called everyone in the club, all of their friends, and even the township and state police to tell them to be on the lookout for any trouble. Dad had strict instructions to call Mom when he left for class, when he arrived, when he left class, and when he got home.

Dad just took it all in and hoped for the best. When the big night came, Dad would be ready.

Before Mom left for Maryland, she put everything on the kitchen table that she thought he needed for his first class. There was a leash, a training collar, poop bags, a jug of water, a water bowl, and a big bag of goodies.

When Dad got home from work, he fed all the dogs, let them out to do their business, and put Vanah and Pandora in their crates for the evening. Having packed everything in the truck, Dad loaded Brooks in the back and sped off for class. It wasn't a long trip, about ten miles, but the whole way, Dad kept thinking there was something he had forgotten.

Leash, goodies, poop bags, water. I guess I have everything.

The further he got away from home, the less he thought about it. Too bad he couldn't hear the telephone ringing off the hook back at the house. I wonder who that could have been.

Upon arrival at the Ritchlandtown Fire Hall for class, Dad was a little uneasy. The class consisted of four other dogs: a golden, an Aussie, an Afghan, and a pug. He appeared to be the only rookie handler of the bunch, but after observing many of Shemp and Vanah's classes over the years, he knew enough to fit right in without too much trouble.

Since Brooks was so good at breed competition, he was a natural at obedience work, which made Dad look all the better. Even though the exercises were rudimentary at best, dealing mainly with sits, stays, and comes, they performed them with such confidence that you would have thought they belonged in the advanced class.

By the end of the evening, they had grasped the lessons so well that the instructor told Dad the only thing he needed to work on was learning his left from his right. Other than that, they seemed to be mastering things that took some dogs and handlers months and sometimes years to accomplish. They were becoming a team. Even Sharon, who had come in late and observed them unnoticed from behind a fire truck, said that they were naturals. An everlasting bond was formed that night between them. Brooks totally enjoyed working for Dad, and Dad got a thrill out of the experience as well. Brooks had truly become Dad's dog.

The trip home that night was a happy one. Dad was so proud of his boy that he even stopped off at McDonald's and bought him a quarter-pounder with cheese. However, the closer they got to home, the more Dad felt that he had forgotten something. Just after they got home and settled down, the phone rang.

"Oh crap!" Dad shouted as he smacked his forehead with his palm. "I forgot to pay the phone bill." What he had really forgotten was to call his wife.

As it turned out, Mom really wasn't that angry after all. Sharon had called her before Dad got home that night and told her about the wonderful class. Sharon said she was looking forward to handling Brooks, since she had never worked with a Tervuren. She mentioned that there was a key show in Harrisburg in a couple of weeks, and she expected a number of Tervs to be showing there.

Brooks needed seven points for his championship. He also needed a major, which meant he had to win in a show that had at least three Tervs. The Harrisburg show would have at least that many Tervs, since it was considered a top show in the area. It was a no-brainer. Brooks had to enter. It was a golden opportunity to score big, and Sharon was able to get an entry in at the last moment to secure a place in the ring.

Chapter 9
Number-One Baby

Sharon knew showing Brooks in Maryland or northern Virginia would court disaster. No one would show if they knew Jashes Atticus of Ubar was entered in the show.

Dad and Sharon shared the same logic that if Brooks was such a threat to the other Tervs when they competed, why not enter their dogs and let the chips fall where they may. If he won, he'd be out of their hair all the sooner. It was not rocket science, but politics and common sense never mix. Fire must be fought with fire.

Sharon had a plan. She was betting that some of the entrees would know nothing about Brooks, since he had never competed in Pennsylvania. The gamble was to show up at the last possible second so no one would think he was there. If any of the dogs he'd competed against showed up, they might let the others know about him. If so, Jashes would be going home empty handed. It was risky, but what choice did they have? Game on.

Harrisburg was close enough to Blooming Glen that Mom and Dad didn't have to get a hotel. It was only a two-hour drive, and it was no big deal to get Brooks there by ten in the morning. His class was scheduled to show around noon, and they would get him there two hours in advance with ample time to meet up with Sharon, allow her to work him a bit, and brush him out a little to get him into show form.

The dogs usually got ready in an area behind the rings. All they had to do was prep the dog and go right into the ring without having to go too far. Brooks had to remain undercover in another part of the building until the last possible second. After his final brushing, Dad took his boy

29

behind the obedience rings in the far side of the arena and waited for Sharon to get him.

It was like *Mission Impossible*. Dad was exhilarated by the intrigue. He didn't know that breed shows could be so much fun until he was brought back to reality. The woman standing next to them with a Pekinese complimented him on having such a handsome dog, but she turned out to be a guy. It was turning out to be an interesting show indeed.

Hurry up, Sharon, and get me out of here.

Sharon appeared and said, "We're in business. Four dogs entered, and they're all from the North. Let's go see our boy strut his stuff." She took Brooks to the ring, and Dad headed to the bleachers to watch with Mom.

There were five Tervs in all. Brooks was the third to go through the preliminary phases of the judging. When all the dogs lined up to do their first passes, he appeared to be in second place.

Ferra, a beautiful mahogany-and-black female who happened to be the number-one Tervuren in the state, occupied the first position.

Sharon pulled out all the tricks she knew to show off his best features as they paraded around the ring, but nothing she did would change the mind of the judge. Would it be his first defeat?

Dad was oblivious to the nuances of conformation. Every time there was a shift in the action, he said, "How are we doing now?"

Coming to the final pass, Mom fell back in her seat and shook her head. "It doesn't look good."

"No!" Dad yelled as he rose from his seat. He was ready to give the judge a piece of his mind, but Mom grabbed his shirttail and pulled him back to his seat. "Don't you dare," she screeched. "You aren't at a ballgame. Sit your ass down now!"

He reluctantly obeyed and continued to watch in utter disappointment.

Ferra and her handler arrogantly pressed forward in their march to first place, relishing the moment. Only one more pass, and victory would be theirs. What happened next had to be seen to be believed.

Brooks seemed to be aware that he was in second place, and he sensed that Sharon had done everything in her power to make him look like the champion he should be. He was not a happy Terv, and this was uncharted water for him. There had never been a dog ahead of him in any competition. Something told him that he had better do something quickly, since this was the last pass.

For Brooks, second place was simply first loser. He looked out the corner of his eye as he pranced around, watching for the moment when the judge would look away. Just one single moment was all he needed to make his move. With every step he took, he moved a little closer to the bitch who was stealing his glory. When the judge turned his head to view the rest of the field, Brooks forged forward and nosed Ferra's butt.

When she let out a yelp, the judge turned back to see what was going on. By that time, Brooks was back in position, showing off his proud gait, head held high and looking good.

Ferra's handler struggled to get her girl back on track, but it was too late.

When the field lined up in front of Judge Mort D. Gottis, he pointed to Brooks and shouted, "You're number one!"

Dad jumped out of his seat, even higher than when the Orioles won the championship in 1983. Fist high in the air, he yelled, "Number one, baby!"

Coming out of the ring, Sharon couldn't believe what had just happened. In all the years that she had handled dogs, she had never witnessed another dog with such a desire to win. The win in Harrisburg made Brooks a legend in Dad's heart and the hearts of all who witnessed his performance. Dad never went to another breed show with Brooks or any other dog.

Ferra's handler argued that Brooks had committed a foul and should have been disqualified, but it fell on deaf ears. It was ruled incidental contact, and the judge's decision to place Brooks first was deemed final.

Harrisburg netted him four points, three shy of the fifteen he needed for the title. Brooks showed three more times, two with Sharon, and got his final point with Don.

After they celebrated his new title, Dad set his sights on other things that he wanted for Brookie. Harrisburg would always remain special to Dad, and any other show was just another show.

Some years later, Dad ran into Sharon and they reminisced about Harrisburg.

Sharon said that whenever she went to Harrisburg, she remembered his performance that spring day with fond memories. About a year later, she met up with the judge at Harrisburg and asked if he remembered the stunning young male Tervuren who upset the number-one female in Pennsylvania.

"Yes, I remembered it well." The grief he got from Ferra's handler never stopped, but he stood by his decision and would do it again if he ever were put in the same position.

Sharon asked why he gave Brooks the win, knowing the other dog had clearly beaten him.

"Did she? I had both dogs dead-even going into the final pass as I recollect. Only one dog could occupy the first position. In their final pass, I could only assume there was contact due to the closeness of the two dogs, nothing more. The fact that the male retained his composure gave me a reason to place him first."

"Seemed like a reasonable explanation to me," Sharon said.

The judge softly added, "All things being equal, I could tell that male knew what was going on and just wanted it more." He gave her a wink and walked away.

"That's what made that day so special," Sharon explained. "Brooks wanted to make me look good. Dogs like that only come once in a lifetime, Jim. Cherish the time you have with him, and he'll always be with you."

As time went by, Dad took Sharon's advice. He stored every memory in his heart, knowing that they would get him through any tough times ahead.

Chapter 10
Dad, You're a Trip

While Brooks pursued the drive for his championship, Dad continued going to obedience class with him to prepare for his next endeavor, earning a title in obedience.

CD, short for companion dog, was the first of three titles a dog would earn in the quest to become a fully titled obedience dog. Obedience competition was totally different from breed, or conformation as it was formally known.

It didn't matter what the dog looked like; it was how it behaved and performed in a series of exercises that earned the title. Sits, stays, heeling, and coming on command were the root of the various drills that culminated in a five-minute sit-stay with the handler out of site. Points were given for how well the exercises were performed; two hundred points was a perfect score. One hundred and seventy was the minimum to qualify, and they had to qualify—or as they say in the business, get a leg—in three shows to earn a title.

Beginners' class would carry on for six weeks. Dad and Brooks never missed a session. Brooks gave 100 percent effort and then some. His focus during the heeling exercises was reminiscent of the border collies Dad so greatly admired. Don't ever tell any Tervuren that we are being compared to those guys. As far as we're concerned, we can do everything they can do just as well if not better. We just don't bounce off walls when we aren't exercised. What's up with that?

Brooks learned the routines well—sometimes too well—and would try to anticipate the next move before the command was given. At times, Dad would get his left confused with his right, totally blowing the exercise. On one occasion, Dad was working Brooks with heeling off lead.

33

With his dog sitting attentively by his left side, commonly known as a sit-stay in heeling position, the instructor commanded them to go forward.

"Heel," Dad instructed.

Brooks immediately forged forward, keeping his eyes focused on Dad. Rigidly, they marched ahead five steps with Brooks tight to his dad's side.

The instructor said, "Left turn."

Brooks correctly turned left, but Dad went right.

After two or three steps, Brooks stopped square in his tracks and looked over his shoulder. *One of these days, he's gonna get it right.*

Dad kept on walking until the trainer said, *"Dummkopf."*

To Dad, it meant, "Your dog showed you up again, dummy."

Peg was the beginner instructor. Don't even ask me what her last name was, since I can't even pronounce it, let alone spell it. She was of German or Dutch descent, but nobody ever knew it, since her Jersey attitude more than covered up her accent. She often used German to express herself. She liked Dad and Brooks and often remarked to Mom about what a nice team they were turning out to be.

Peg used Brooks a lot in demonstrating new exercises. In several instances, she singled them out as a team when they would grasp a concept she was teaching.

Not to let it get to Dad's head, she would always say, "I'll make you great—despite the fact that you're a *dummkopf.*" But then again, everyone was a *dummkopf* in her eyes.

Dad continued going to the beginner's class, and Vanah and Mom worked in the intermediate class that followed. Toward the end of the six weeks, Peg started to allow Brooks and Dad to participate just to get the feel for what they were going to get into when they graduated. The main differences between the two classes were that there were more dogs in the intermediate class, and the class was ongoing, meaning there was no beginning or end. Anyone could participate as long as they had graduated from the beginner class.

A normal night would have eight to ten teams participating; the big problem with the class was that some nights, especially before a big trial, as many as twenty dogs and handlers all came out to get some work in. This made it tough for the rookie dogs, since they weren't used to working around so many teams. The individualized instruction wasn't the same.

Graduation night for Brooks and Dad happened to be on the eve of a major obedience trial. Beginner's class started on time, and Peg ran everyone through the warm-up exercises. To pass the class, a team had to go through all the basic movements of a novice trial under control; if the dog didn't take off, they passed.

As the class progressed, the fire hall became progressively filled with handlers who were getting there early for the next class. Peg would always save the best teams for last; in that class, it was Dad and Brooks. By the time they were ready to go through their evaluation, most of the handlers had elected to use their leads to get through the test because there were at least fifteen teams waiting outside the ring.

Peg allowed leads for beginners, as long as it was a loose lead and wasn't used in excess to force the dog through the exercise. Mom and Vanah were there for the next class and for support. Dad didn't know the place would be filled to capacity when it was time for them to be tested.

Mom had a ringside view, and she was relieved to see the rest of the class using leads. Even though Dad loved to show off his boy's ability to work off lead, she didn't think he was stupid enough to work him off lead with so many people around. The amount of room they had to work in wasn't the problem, since the area was the size of an official ring. However, the area wasn't roped off, and the noise posed a distraction for even the best teams. It just wasn't adding up to the ideal night that Dad had envisioned.

With minutes running short for the spring beginners' class of 1993, the time came for our heroes to step up and show what they were made of—even though it was to be on lead.

"Will Jim Loveless and his partner Brooks please take their places," Peg announced.

When they stepped up to the entrance of the ring, Dad placed Brookie in a sit position and waited for the next instruction.

"Heel," Peg said.

What only took a few seconds seemed like an eternity to Mom as she stood outside the ring in anticipation of their performance.

Dad took a moment to scope out all the disorder going on outside the work area. Seeing all the commotion, he looked down and noticed that Brooks was totally focused on Dad and was anxiously awaiting his command. Dad looked over the area one more time and saw Mom mouth, "Don't you dare." His hand had moved down the lead and was poised at Brooks's collar for a quick release. Mom's warning was all he needed to pop the release.

It wasn't textbook, and the fact that they were glued together the whole way through the first exercise didn't help with their style points, but they were working without the leash. All went well besides the occasional left when they were supposed to go right.

I think the NASCAR in Dad made him always want to turn left.

The big challenge was the sit and stay. All the dogs were lined up, put in a sit, and told to stay. This was an advanced exercise, but Peg had her beginners learn it anyway. She believed it made for good control in the group exercises they would have to perform if they were to compete.

What's so hard about that? The handlers are told to leave and remain out of sight for five minutes. The dogs can stand up or lie down, but they can't leave the spot where they were left. If they moved, it was an immediate disqualification. If there was anything Dad was most afraid of, it was this.

Brooks was quite the ladies' man, and he tended to flirt with the girls when he was left alone. Just about every time he was placed next to a lady dog, he would try to make out with her. He couldn't help it if he was attracted to the opposite sex, but it drove Dad crazy each time he'd go out of sight for the exercise. In a few moments, the instructor would say, "Brooks is up." Time and time again, it would happen. If a guy dog was next to him, no problem. It was the girls who he couldn't resist. It was definitely a problem they had to work on, but for now, they just had to get through the evaluation.

It was good that Brooks and Dad were the last team to perform. They didn't have to leave the ring. When the others were called back for the sit-stay exercise, Brooks was placed between two males. The command was given to sit the dogs, and the handlers walked to the far end of the ring and faced them from about thirty feet away. After thirty seconds or so, Dad and the rest of his cohorts were escorted to the far side of the hall, out of sight, but within earshot of any instructions from the ring.

Dad's concern was with all the commotion generated by the teams arriving for the next class. Twice as many people and dogs were present than normal, and that spelled trouble for the inexperienced dogs waiting for their masters to return. It seemed that if time went by any slower, they'd be in reverse.

Nervously, the teams paced behind the fire trucks, peeking through the windows to try to get a look at how their companions were doing. One, two, three minutes passed, and all seemed well. There was the occasional butt shift from hip to hip, scratch of the ear, or lying down, but all held their ground. It was a beautiful thing.

Just as the fourth minute ticked away, the unbelievable happened. The ear-piercing wail of the siren blared like never before, and it scared the crap out of everyone within fifty feet. The reverb shook the building like an earthquake. The unexpected suddenness sent dogs scrambling, and stunned the humans.

Dad and his classmates had been lulled into a false state of complacency prior to the eruption. There was less than a minute to go before the ultimate taste of conquest could be savored. Dad was sitting on the running board of engine five when the siren blasted him straight up, driving his head into the bell that protruded from the truck. That must have hurt.

The siren had gone off many times in the past, but it sounded louder and went on for what seemed to be an eternity. To make matters worse, the hall was filled to more than twice its normal capacity, which added to the hysteria.

While Dad tried to gain his composure, everyone else rushed to the ring to retrieve his or her dog. The scene resembled the end of the parade in *Animal House*.

Peg screamed, "Be calm! Be calm!"

Dogs and handlers scurried back and forth. When Dad finally forced his way to what was left of the ring, all the dogs had taken off. The masters were trying to chase them down. Even Vanah had split, taking Mom out to the parking lot to get her.

The horn was wailing away when Dad found Brooks in the spot where he had been left.

Brooks was howling like a prairie dog. By the time he made it over to his boy, the commotion had subsided. Everyone was taking inventory of the dogs and positions. The siren slowly echoed away, but Brookie tried to make up for the loss of decibels by shrieking even louder. With his head pointing straight up in the air, he sounded off like a siren, drawing everyone's attention.

Dad knelt down in front of Brooks and hugged him like he never had before. He stood up and commanded the dog to heel. Brooks did as he was told.

The lone dog and handler overcame the uproar and accepted the long applause of their companions. Dad said, "You're a trip, Brookie." It would not be the last time he said that.

When Dad attended the next class, a fireman approached and handed him an old Phillies cap. "I'm guessing this is yours. We found it hooked to the clapper in the bell on truck five. Since you're the only dude in here, and judging by the lump on your forehead, I'm guessing it belongs to you."

Brooks thought, *Dad, you're a trip.* It wasn't the last time he thought that.

Chapter 11
Gone to the Dogs

It had been three months since Brooks had arrived on the scene, and already he was making a name for himself—and Dad too. They were taking the Hilltown Dog Training Club by storm and fast becoming rising stars in the dog obedience world that they were now a part of.

The wonderful world of sports and model trains that Dad so passionately loved from the past had transformed into a life of obedience classes and fun matches. Our heroes were now a team, constantly taking advantage of any opportunity to get some ring time in preparation for their first show. It wasn't so much that Dad was that ambitious about training; Mom pushing him got him off his ass and to the backyard to work on heeling and staying. Class was fun, and practice was a bore. But practice was a must to carry over what they learned in order to do well in the trials. With class on Tuesdays, matches on the weekends, and practice in between, there was little time for anything else.

With the first trial coming up in a couple of weeks, Dad needed a break. Mom had heard that there was a match being held just north of Baltimore, and she thought it might be nice to take Vanah and Brooks to see what was going on back in the old neighborhood.

It was the first long trip for Vanah and Brooks. They rode together to class from time to time—but never on a drive over twenty miles. Dad loaded up the Bronco, and Mom had to bring everything she could think of. X-pens, mats, leashes, toys, food, and water were the normal fare for the dogs, but a crate, beds, tarps, and more toys were added to the inventory just in case.

They were only going down for the day—not staying for a month! All that stuff was for the dogs, and that didn't count the chairs, camp table, and cooler. And there was Mom's stuff. Dad taught me to never question what a woman brings on a trip. He said, "Just shut up and deal with it." That was rule two; you'll learn rule one in a minute. Three bags, two blankets, three coats, and a purse that was the size of a duffel bag filled the rest of the cargo area. Then it was time for the dogs. Vanah had first dibs, staking her place in the back behind her mommy, and Brooks camped out behind Dad.

Once everyone was in place, Dad reviewed everything he had loaded. Having been a pilot from many years, he checked his preparations for a trip with Mom like a preflight inspection when he was taking off to the wild blue yonder. "Gas, check. Oil, check. Mirrors, check. Ignition on, contact." He was reliving his glory days when he took to the skies in his Piper 140. He was a regular Walter Mitty. The only difference was that he actually did the things he daydreamed about.

Out of the driveway and down the road they went, trucking to the sounds of the Hollies and "Long Cool Woman in a Black Dress." Life couldn't be better; the weather was nice, the roads were clear, and they were off to their favorite town. Just as things couldn't get any better, they approached the interstate.

Mom moaned, "We have to go back."

"What?" Dad cried out.

"I forgot Vanah's good collar," she exclaimed. "We have to go back and get it."

"No! No, no, no, no," he said as he made an illegal U-turn in front of the toll plaza. "You do this to me every time!"

Mom pressed back in her seat, crossed her arms, and looked out the window. "If you hadn't rushed me, I could have made sure not to have left it behind."

Dad knew better than to argue; now you know rule one.

Time passes slowly when you're pissed, and the twenty-minute delay seemed like an hour.

Vanah and Brooks knew that when Mom and Dad weren't talking, rule three was now in effect—behave when the parents are mad at each other.

Once out on the interstate, Brooks decided to break the ice by howling to the tune on the radio. The song was "Me and You and a Dog Named Boo." Something about the word boo got to him. Mom looked back and started to laugh.

Dad peered back through the rearview mirror and chimed in with his own wail. Before they knew it, everyone was singing and tooling down I-95. All was right with the world again.

The trip took less than two hours, and Dad was amazed that Mom didn't ask for her usual pit stop. They never traveled more than fifty miles without the familiar request for a stop. It was her way of apologizing for the screw-up at the beginning of the trip, but she would never come out and say she had done anything wrong. The fourth rule was to take what you can get and like it. You gotta love her.

The event was being held at the state fairgrounds in Timonium, Maryland, just north of Baltimore. It was a place that was very familiar for Dad since back in the day; he used to have a very successful business custom-painting and selling model trains. He had gained quite a bit of respect and fame from his fellow model railroaders at a spring train show a couple of years back. They had been displaced from the spacious exhibition hall where they usually held the show and were bumped to the lowly Cow Palace, a bare-bones building in a forgotten corner of the complex. Sales plummeted as a result, but someone found a stray cat and let it loose in the breed ring, causing total pandemonium throughout the exhibition hall. Business never picked up, but no one could deny the huge smiles that broke out on the faces of the beleaguered merchants who witnessed the spectacle.

At the end of the show, when the receipts were tallied, only one exhibitor showed an increase in profits from the previous year. Dad's cash box held $752.25 and a "Vote for Ronnie" button.

When Mom, Dad, and the dogs pulled into the parking lot for the dog show, they were greeted by a sign for the train show in the Cow Palace. Dad's face turned red as a caboose.

Chapter 12
The Revelation

The dog show was hosted by the Oriole Dog Training Club, which had no affiliation with the baseball team, much to Dad's dismay. It was the same group that had implicated him in the "Great Cat Caper" as it came to be known, but it was never actually proven that he had anything to do with it.

Dad had totally forgotten about the incident; otherwise, he never would have agreed to come that weekend, especially since the train show attendees were probably plotting another coup. In the exhibition hall, a big white sign warned everyone to beware of stray cats.

Throughout the event, Dad kept his collar up and his hat down over his eyes when milling around. It really wasn't necessary though; the place was so crowded that it was doubtful anyone would recognize him. Brooks and he did fairly well in the obedience match, scoring a career low in missed directions, blowing only one left turn.

Vanah and Mom also scored high, notching their best showing of the season. Once they finished their runs, it was time to relax and check out the various vendors and exhibits that were spread out over the venue.

From leashes to toys and pens to food, this place had it all for the most discriminating dog handler. Being fairly green behind the gills in this big bold world of canines, Dad was utterly amazed by what was available. Stumbling upon a nicely decorated table next to the snack bar, he ate one of the Christmas tree cookies.

"Not bad," he remarked. "Not bad at all. A little chewy, but all in all, not bad."

Noticing that he was reaching for another, Mom elbowed him hard in the ribs and whispered, "Just what do you think you're doing? Those are dog cookies, you doofus!"

"Nom they aren't," he quipped. "They're Christmas cookies. See how they're so nicely iced and all."

Rolling her eyes, she took a huge sigh and said, "Sometimes I think the dogs are smarter than you. In fact, I know it. Haven't you ever heard of gourmet dog cookies?" Smacking his outreached hand away from the tray of goodies, she remarked, "That's what you just ate."

At last report, Dad was swilling down hot coffee, thinking it would kill anything bad that was in the treats.

Brooks and Vanah were quietly minding their own business on lead. Looking down at them, Mom remarked, "If you guys could only talk. I just can't make this stuff up, but who'd believe me?"

Once Dad was convinced he was going to live—and after he downed a few Red Hots for good measure—they were off to the outdoor exhibits to see what was going on. The herding and tracking demonstrations did nothing for them.

Having their fill for the day, it was time to get their gear and head for the hills. As they made their way across the grounds, Mom noticed something going on in the infield of the old trotter track. A number of tents were set up around a fenced-in area. They noticed all kinds of obstacles spread out inside the ring and a border collie running.

When they got up to the sideline, Brooks noticed other dogs outside the fencing jumping over hurdles and scurrying around under the control of their handlers and off lead. With his head spinning, trying to take in all that was going on around him, Brooks erupted, barking and carrying on like a mad man. No dog in the history of mankind has had a more intimidating growl than Brooks Robinson Loveless. His outbreak carried over the venue like an atomic explosion, sending the dog running the course into the fence in bewilderment. The spectators and teams that were surrounding the demonstration scrambled to gain control of their pets, being totally caught off guard by the uproar.

As suddenly as Brooks exploded, he stopped. All eyes were on them.

Mom was mortified, slowly backing away and trying to look like an innocent bystander. "You're on your own with this one," she muttered under her breath.

Feeling like a smacked ass, what could Dad do? His dog had disrupted whatever they were doing, and he was totally dismayed by what they might say or do. As he tried to conjure up some kind of apology, a short, attractive, middle-aged lady with a very athletic look sprinted across the ring toward them.

"You're dead," Mom mumbled. "You're so dead it isn't funny."

The woman said, "Hi. I'm Terry."

Dad squeaked in a high-pitched, half clearing of his throat. "I'm humiliated. I mean, my name is Jim."

"Nice to meet you, and your Tervuren's name is?"

Looking down at his smiling Terv, he replied, "Mud."

Laughing at his answer, she knelt down and put her hand out to let him give her the once-over. Gaining his approval, she began scratching under his chin. "Well, Mister Mud, you pack quite a punch with that bark of yours." She chuckled. "I trust you approve of our little demonstration?"

Feeling the relief from Terry's good nature, Dad responded, "Actually, his name is Brooks, and I have to apologize for our actions. We were curious about what all this was, and I guess we should have approached with a little more care."

She led them over to a tent where everyone seemed to be congregating. "Happens all the time. We actually train with distractions to keep the dogs focused while running a course. Your Brooks just was a little more amplified than what these guys are used to. But that's okay; we need the experience."

Seeing that things were under control, Mom came out from hiding.

Dad introduced her and Vanah to Terry.

"This is dog agility, isn't it?" Mom asked.

"Yes, that's exactly what it is," responded Terry. "We have several Tervurens like yours in the club, and they do very well. Are you interested in joining?"

Mom explained her interest and quizzed Terry about the sport.

Dad and Brooks made their way over to the now unoccupied ring and started examining all the equipment, board by board and nail by nail. Though Mom's attention was focused on participation, it was obvious where Dad's mind was: in a shop, building all those very cool obstacles.

They realized how late it was getting, and that agility offered something for both of them. Mom had seen it on TV and heard people talking about it at the club, but this was the first time she had experienced it live.

Dad got acquainted with the guy who managed all the equipment while Mom and Van were being shown how the obstacles worked. Even though he was interested in participating, the fun of building all this equipment was foremost in his mind.

Mom and Dad were really excited about this new sport. As they walked back to the Bronco, they were batting ideas back and forth about what this new venture meant to them. It had been a great day with success in the ring and out.

Just as they passed by the exhibition hall, they heard a loud commotion inside the building. A side door opened, and a woman barreled out like a running back charging through the line for a touchdown. She was on a mission, looking for someone to kill!

"That's Edna Goldfinch," Mom exclaimed. "She's the chairperson for the show. She taught my obedience class when I had Shemp."

Scurrying over to greet her, Mom said, "Hi, Edna. Great show you put on."

"Oh hi, Leslie. It would be a great show if I didn't have to deal with morons. I'm sorry. I just get so exasperated sometimes. Ever since we booted those train show guys to the Cow Palace a few years back, they always want to disrupt our show by letting a stray cat in the building. It's become a ritual to them."

Dad was standing right behind Mom.

Edna added, "If I only could catch the jackass that started this, and I will, I'll string him up, skin his hide, and use it for dog food."

Dad tried to fade out of range of the enraged madwoman's dragnet.

"Wait a minute," Edna proclaimed as she stepped between Mom and Dad. "I know who you are."

Mom gulped. *This is it. All this work with the dogs down the drain. I'll never be able to face my friends back at the club ever again.*

"You're the owner of Jashes," she proclaimed. "I saw how your handler worked him in Harrisburg—or shall I say how he worked her."

Dad cleared his throat and said, "You did?"

Edna knelt down and motioned to Brooks to come over. As Brookie nuzzled his new friend, Edna continued, "A lot of us were at that show.

45

I have to tell you he's quite a dog. You made quite a name for yourself at that show if you didn't know it by now."

Gaining confidence with every word, Dad responded, "He's doing very well in obedience too, I might add."

"If he's as good at that as he was in conformation, you have quite a dog on your hands. Gotta go. I'm on a mission to find out who's responsible for all these shenanigans. Good luck with your dog, and I hope to see you around some more."

Breathing a great sigh of relief, Mom and Dad decided not to press their luck and hurried back to their vehicle. After getting everything packed in, Dad fired up the Bronco and peeled past the ever-growing commotion at the exhibition hall. "The train boys must have outdone themselves this year," he said jokingly.

As they sped out the gate, he couldn't help but view the scene of chaos and carnage out the rearview mirror. Dad the train guy had turned into Dad the dog guy. Motoring up the interstate to Pennsylvania, he said, "As we slowly fade into the sunset, we say farewell, Hiawatha, till another day."

Hiawatha was Timonium, and there would never be another day like that one.

Chapter 13
The Time Has Come

With their trip to Timonium behind them, it was back to work in preparing for the upcoming obedience trials. Mom had entered herself and Van along with Dad and Brooks in three shows that were coming up in less than a month, and that meant not missing any classes and lots of practice in between.

Their first night back to class could have been dubbed show-and-tell night as both spun yarns of their heroic acts defending each other from the warring factions between trains and dogs. Mom fended off the hordes that wanted to string Dad up for his past deeds with the train show, and Dad protected Mom by beating back the throngs. The innocent bystanders were polite enough to listen. Brooks and Vanah quietly sat by their respective hero and rolled their eyes at each other, knowing that only they knew the real truth.

It was hard for both to get the experience they had with the agility people totally out of their heads. The fast-paced excitement and competitiveness of the sport boiled over in their minds, casting a shadow of dullness over obedience competition.

They were committed to this, and both were going to see it through. They knew a dog and handler with good obedience skills definitely had the advantage in agility competition. Nonetheless, they tucked the thoughts in the back of their minds and only brought them to the forefront as inspiration for getting the titles sooner.

Returning to class was tough enough for Mom since she hadn't worked Vanah in three days, but it was a different story for Dad. It was his first time in the intermediate group, and the culture shock was a little hard to get used to. There were more than twice the number of dogs, and the amount of one-on-one attention was far less than in beginners. Moreover, they weren't the number-one team as they had been in the past class, and the mistakes they made proved to be embarrassing until they saw that even the most experienced dogs made them too. It was the first time they worked next to Mom and Van, finding it hard to fight off the urge to compete with them. All in all, there was work to be done, but in a short time, they blended in just fine.

It didn't take long for Dad and Brooks to become favorite sons of the class. Dad's easygoing approach and willingness to listen to the instructor and fellow handlers gained him much respect within his group. A sense of humor over his directional misgivings also didn't hurt.

One night, he took quite a ribbing over going right when he was supposed to have gone left, which cost them a qualifying score in a practice match. When Dad went back to the ring for a correctional exercise, he put his shoes on the wrong feet to remind himself to go in the right direction. There were laughs all around when they took a bow for getting it right. So it went: class on Tuesdays, matches on Sundays, and practice in between.

On a rather warm day in early May, Dad and Brooks competed in their very first trial.

Mom, Vanah, and Brooks all had experience in the ring, and it was natural for Dad to be a little nervous. When asked how he felt, Dad responded, "What the hell am I doing here?"

Brooks didn't make it any better by barking at every dog he saw from when they unloaded the gear until they set up just outside of the entrance to the field house.

"That's Brooks letting everyone know he's here to compete," Mom explained as she managed the dogs while Dad set up the crates. "Now, when you get set up, be sure to take him out to do his business. It's very important, and the number-one rule of handling in the ring. If he gets nervous and has an accident, you will be disqualified. Do you hear me?"

Dad had other things running through his mind. "Maybe I should do that wrong shoe on the wrong foot approach to lighten things up," he proposed.

"This is serious stuff here," she reprimanded. "This is a trial, and these judges are serious about how they score you. Get real."

She wasn't getting through to him. When Dad got nervous, he used his sense of humor to calm himself down. "I know this is a trial, and it's for real, but can't I have a little fun?"

"You can have fun after you qualify—if you qualify. Now I have to check us in and then find out where I can watch you guys. Please take care of Brooks and make sure he goes." She hoped he would do as she asked, but she knew he could be as unpredictable as the weather.

Mom wasn't gone five seconds before Dad's preoccupied mind had him wondering how he was going to get through the rigid structure of a trial. Thinking that there was plenty of time to get Brooks squared away, Dad put him in his pen, secured everything, and made his way to the competition area.

The novice competition had already begun. Watching the first team go through the routine, he observed that it was more formal than he was used to. Before, you could joke with ring crew and even the judge. If you screwed up, it was okay. It was only a match, and in some cases, they allowed you to correct yourself.

Here it was all business, and these folks were as competitive as Tiger Woods is about making a five-foot putt to win the Masters. The other thing that was putting a knot in his stomach was that these folks were all seasoned veterans who knew their lefts from their rights. He remained there for some time, hoping to see someone make a major mistake. He did not want to see them fail, but he wanted to see how they reacted to messing up in the ring. It was something he was sure to do, and he didn't want to be the only one.

He was really uneasy about all of it. Six or eight teams had gone through their exercises, and all had nearly perfect scores. There might have been a point off here or there for little missed cues, but it was a tough group to beat. He was somewhat awestruck. It wasn't at all what he had expected. He'd been to the trials before—but only as a fan for Mom and Shemp. It was years ago, and he never had to be concerned about actually competing.

This is my first trial. The hell with first, second, or even third place. I'm just going to have fun, and if the folks here don't like it, then they can kiss my butt.

Just as fast as he built up his confidence to go out there and show them there was another way of doing things, the wrath of Mom struck. Like a tornado brewing up on the plains of Kansas, she appeared at his side. "What are you doing in here? Don't you know you're on deck in three more runs?"

Oh crap. No time to panic now. He ran back through the crowd to get Brooks. *Keep it fun; just keep it fun.*

Mom muttered, "I'll kill him. I'll kill him."

In the pen, Brooks was pacing nervously in anticipation of what was to come. Enough of this standing around—let me out so I can strut my stuff.

Realizing he had less time than he thought to get ready, Dad hadn't taken Mom's advice to allow Brooks to do his business. Brooks was ripe for an accident in the ring. The area that was set aside for the dogs to relieve themselves was in the opposite direction of the ring, and there was simply not enough time to get it done.

Mom had stayed back at the ring in the hopes of buying some time for her absentminded husband who was about to blow his first qualifying attempt at a companion dog title. She broke out in a cold sweat when the ring steward called out, "Number 114, Shetland sheepdog Rory is up, and number 109, Belgian Tervuren Brooks is on deck!"

"Where is Brooks?"

The large crowd of spectators milling about and the many handlers shuffling their dogs between the rings made it particularly hard for anyone in a hurry to get from one place to another. Time was running out for our heroes.

Rory started his routine flawlessly and efficiently, making good use of the time he had in the ring.

As time was growing short, Mom happened to glance over at one of the advanced rings.

Dad and Brooks were heeling back and forth in the small warm up area.

She dashed over and stood in amazement, hands on her hips and ready to kill. "What the hell are you doing? You're in the wrong area, and you are about to be disqualified!" Grabbing the lead from him, she commanded, "I'll take care of Brookie, and you get your dumb ass over there and check in with the steward. She's been calling and calling for you."

As luck would have it, Rory stopped in his tracks while doing his final heeling exercise, arched his back, and raised his tail up and down like he was pumping water. It wasn't water he was pumping; to the embarrassment of his handler, he left the biggest, smelliest dump anybody had ever witnessed in the middle of the ring.

The dog obedience gods were shining down on Dad that afternoon. The break in the action bought Dad some time. He checked in, got his number affixed to his arm, and Brooks was handed to him.

Mom said, "Good luck."

While the cleanup crews were busy removing Rory's exhaust and fumigating the area, Dad grew more nervous. It wasn't about how he was going to remember his right from his left or the ability to keep his dog under control with so much activity going on outside the ring. It was the reminder that he had forgotten to observe Mom's number-one rule. In Dad's warped way of thinking, he wasn't worried so much about Brooks having an accident as he was about Mom asking if he had taken his dog out. He didn't want to lie to her, but he didn't want to endure her wrath over not doing what she had said. He avoided looking over at her and acted preoccupied while awaiting his grand entry into the ring.

With Rory's mishap cleaned up as best as the ring crew could do, they were ready to continue the competition.

The judge took her place just off the center of the ring to get the best view of the team. She was older and tolerated no nonsense or deviation from the rules. It was written all over her face that she didn't like beginners. Though a bit overweight, she maneuvered around the area like a cheetah stalking her prey.

"No hiding any mistakes from this old bird," Dad whispered under his breath.

"I beg your pardon, sir," the gate steward replied in a satirical tone.

"Nothing," he said. "Just talking to myself."

"Please reserve your talk to the commands to your dog. There is no talking in the ring."

"Sorry," he said sheepishly.

It was shaping up to be a bad day. Mom was all over him for not being where he was supposed to be. Brooks hadn't been properly taken care of and was ripe for a dump. The stewards were all over him to shut up. On top of all that, the lingering odor from Rory's poop was starting to lure Brooks into thinking it was okay to duplicate his gesture.

Let's just get this pending disaster over with, and I'll just go back to playing with my model trains. This definitely isn't fun.

As Dad and Brooks stood at the entrance to the ring, awaiting the command to heel his dog, an idea sprang into his head. Just because he was a novice handler didn't mean he was going to let these ring Nazis intimidate him this way. Putting one foot into the ring, he waved his hand in the air and shouted, "Excuse me, Judge!"

It was as if all the lights had gone out and the spotlight was on him.

Mom had made her way behind the exit at the far side of the ring. She turned to a friend and exclaimed, "He's going to get himself disqualified—and in his first trial to boot!"

"Sir?" the judge responded. "Is there a problem?"

"Yes, ma'am. There is. If I could bother you to come over here to witness this smell. I commend the ring crew for doing a fine job, but the odor is a distraction to my dog."

As she made her way to the area of concern, Dad saw a "kink in the old gal's armor."

"Pure ambrosia it is not," she quipped. "Let's get some vinegar, and clear the air. Sir, my apologies."

He looked over at Mom, puffing his chest out and playing the moment like a veteran.

Mom turned to her friend and said, "He's not as dumb as he looks."

Advantage, Dad.

When the judge gave her command to commence, Brooks was totally focused on Dad.

When she said, "Heel," he waited for Brooks to step forward.

With the precision of two drag racers at a green light, they were off. So far, so good as they neared the back of the ring.

The judge said, "Left turn."

Leading slightly with his left leg and pointing his foot in the directions of the turn, Brooks instinctively sensed the direction, and they executed a perfect ninety-degree left turn. Headed to the side of the ring where a number of spectators lined up to watch, Brookie stayed tight to Dad's side as they performed an almost textbook about-turn, leading into a halt. Brooks was marked off for crowding Dad a little, but it was minor. It wasn't really the dog's fault, since Dad's pigeon-toed gait gave that appearance.

They made it through the heeling portion of the competition with amazing ease. The figure eight was not bad, but Brooks was marked off with some lagging, which was unusual for him since he normally forged ahead. The stand for examination was a no-brainer since, Brooks was used to judges giving him the once-over from breed trials. They aced it with no points deducted. Amazingly, both looked like they had been doing this for years.

Mom was astonished by Dad's composure and calm, considering how nervous he had been.

There was one more exercise to be performed before breaking for the sit-stays. At first, Dad was looking forward to the recall, since they did it best.

When the judge instructed Dad about where to place Brooks for the exercise, it was apparent that he would have to pass over the area that had been soiled by Rory. Even though the area had been cleaned up a second time, there was always the chance he'd pick up some lingering scent that would distract him as he passed by.

If it had been me, I might have marked the area to show I had been there! Don't ask me why we do these things. It's just our way of saying, "Kilroy was here." If I hadn't gone in a while and I was looking to get some relief, what better place to go than where another dog had gone.

It had been several hours since Brooks had any relief, and that was foremost on Dad's mind when he placed him in a sit-stay. Thinking quickly, Dad left his boy and walked way to the right of the accident scene in the hopes that Brooks would follow his path when recalled. Stopping at the required twenty-five feet away, he turned and faced his dog as far to the right as he could without being charged with being out of position.

Mom knew just what was going on and was amazed by Dad's presence in the ring. She tightly grasped the rope that surrounded the ring and gripped it tight in anticipation of what was to come.

"Call your dog," the judge instructed.

Dad said, "Brooks, come."

Brooks hesitated for a second and looked at Dad.

By rule, all Dad could do was stand in a recall—no clapping hands or using body gestures to encourage the dog. He just had to stand there with his hands by his sides, using only the inflection of his voice to punctuate the command.

The seconds ticked by like minutes as Brooks sat there like his butt had been cemented to the floor.

Dad fought the urge to use his hands or change position to encourage the dog.

Just as the judge was about to issue a second command to call his dog, which would cost them points, Brooks reared up and shot down the ring like he was coming for dinner. He stopped in front of Dad as if he was sporting disk brakes. He recoiled into a perfect heel position on Dad's command.

The judge said, "Exercise finished."

Though they got a slight deduction in points for the delay in the recall, Brooks evaded the accident area that Dad had been so concerned about and avoided disqualification. There was no explanation for his slow reaction other than he was trying to figure out why Dad seemed unconfident that his boy wouldn't perform the exercise. After all, this was their favorite exercise.

Dad almost outsmarted himself by not trusting his dog, and he came close to costing him dearly, a lesson he never forgot.

The first part of the competition was over, and they had managed to get through it with only a few points deducted. Before rewarding Brooks with goodies, they went to the relief area. Returning to his crate, Brooks was handsomely rewarded with his favorite treat, Oinker Roll, a kind of pork bologna Mom cut up in little dime-sized pieces. It was a canine delight for sure.

Chapter 14
The Payoff

It was time for the combined group exercise, better known as "Sits and Downs." There were two parts to this exercise; first was the long sit. The dogs would be lined up as a group about five feet apart. On command, they were put in a sit, and the handler had to go to the other side of the ring and face the dog. For one agonizing minute, the dogs had to remain in their sit until the handlers returned and were given the "exercise finished" command.

The second part was the same as the first except the dogs were placed in a down position and had to remain there for three minutes. It had to be performed with nine other dogs and lots of noise and distractions outside the ring. Depending on the circumstances, it could tax even the most experienced teams, but Dad took the exercise very seriously.

As the handlers were called to the ring, Dad and Brooks were more prepared than the first time. Brooks had done his business and seemed eager to perform, especially since they had done so well in the earlier round.

Mom had given Dad some coaching and had determined that he was second from the end and would be positioned between a German shepherd and a golden retriever, two well-behaved dogs. Thank God the golden was the buffer between a yapping miniature pinscher and an exuberant poodle. Both had nonqualifying scores in the early going but were expected to do the sits and downs to complete their runs. That was the gamble that made this round tough or easy, and Brooks seemed to have been dealt a good hand for this one.

The teams assembled at the entrance to the ring, and it seemed that the real challenge to this exercise was entering the ring. It was early afternoon, and all the rings in the arena were up and running. The aisles were choked with people trying to get their dogs to and from their assignments and many spectators. It was "pure pandalerium," as Jeff Foxworthy would say.

Just outside the entry gate, Brooks was raring to go, but they were to be next to the last going in.

As Brooks sat there patiently, a mother with a young boy in a stroller happened by. The kid had a hot dog in his hand. When they approached, the boy looked at a border collie. Insulted that the other dog got the attention, Brooks snagged the hot dog when the boy wasn't looking. Fast and clean was his motto when it came to swiping food, and the child never knew what happened.

They were halfway past the ring before they knew what had happened; by then, the evidence was long gone. When Dad looked down at Brooks, he stopped chewing. When Dad looked away, the chewing resumed. Suspicious that something was up, Dad looked again, and the chewing stopped. The third time was the charm when he discovered mustard on his chin. Before he could figure out what was going on, they were called to the ring.

I'm not sure whether Dad ever realized what was going on, but it didn't matter; they had to get through the final exercises to earn their first leg on their way to an obedience title.

Ten dogs were lined up at the back of the ring, roughly five feet apart. Dad and Brooks were second from the end; the golden retriever was next to the misbehaving poodle.

The ring stewards took their positions to maintain order, and the judge paced from right to left, hands folded behind her. She reviewed the procedures so there would be no confusion. Taking her position to be able to view each and every participant, she instructed the handlers to place their armbands behind their dogs.

Surprisingly, the German shepherd decided to become a little playful. Breaking from her sit, she grabbed her handler's armband and took off down the ring. She hurdled the rope and ran into the crowd, searching for someone she knew. The horrified handler and two stewards followed in pursuit.

Having little tolerance for these kinds of things, the judge commanded everyone to spread out to fill the void since the young shepherd would not be returning.

Dad and Brooks were on the outside, next to the aisle that led to the great outdoors. There was nothing they could do but hope and pray that Brooks would focus on the job at hand and leave the outside world alone for a few lousy minutes.

With everyone in place, the judge asked, "Handlers ready? Sit your dog."

All the dogs went down in a sit with a variable degree of ease.

"Leave your dog," the judge said.

Each dog was left to wonder when its handler would return. Once everyone had made it to the opposite side of the ring, they all turned to face the dogs.

The clock began to tick off sixty seconds. Amazingly, the exercise went off without a hitch. All the dogs stayed put, including the poodle and pinscher who everyone figured would break.

"Back to your dogs. Exercise finished."

It was a flawless performance by all.

Dad began to feel a little more confident in how Brooks handled being on the end and ignored all the outside distractions. After one more performance, the first leg to a title would be theirs. The same procedure faced them in the down exercise; the only difference was that the dog would lie down for a grueling three minutes.

"Handlers ready? Down your dog," the judge commanded. "Leave your dog."

The anxiety began.

About two minutes into the exercise, all seemed well. Brooks remained steady as a rock, shifting from one elbow to the other. He held his position. Just when things couldn't get any better, lightning struck.

"That's the dog that took my hot dog," a boy screeched. The boy was standing about three feet away. He had broken away from his stroller and was about to enter the ring.

Brooks just rolled on his side and placed the kid on ignore. It was his way of saying, "Get away from me, son. You bother me."

A steward rushed over and carefully stood between the dog and the boy, trying not to be disruptive. Unfortunately for the poodle, the pinscher, and one other dog at the far end, they all broke from their downs. The child was quickly subdued.

"Back to your dog," the judge said. "Exercise finished."

They had done it. High-fives all around; the thrill of victory and the agony of defeat had begun.

Mom rushed to the ring to give hugs to Brookie and Dad. "It was a hard-fought victory, but the team prevailed," Dad proclaimed, sounding like Knute Rockne giving a victory speech. "We went out there and fought for every point, looked adversity square in the eye and spat in it. We—"

"Cool it, hotshot," Mom said. "It's only one leg toward your title. You have two more to go." *Good god. Lord forbid! What he's going to be like when he does get their title?*

Brooks took it all in stride, enjoying all the pats on the back and the Oinker Roll.

Yes, indeed. Dad always seemed to go from the sublime to the ridiculous. The victory lap around the ring was a bit much, but he did have the right to celebrate. He'd accomplished a lot in the short few months. He had gone from knowing absolutely nothing about handling dogs to receiving his first leg in his quest to win a companion dog title for his boy. It wasn't the title, but it was their first success. Mom knew that there was something special about the first one. She would always remember her first one.

That night, it was rib eye steaks on the grill for all. For Brooks, it was the bone to chew on and the satisfaction that he was finally appreciated.

With their first trial behind them, they earned their second leg at Ambler. It wasn't the best showing. Dad was back to his usual misdirection antics, but the judge was more than lenient, and they qualified in the top five. Though he knew he had gotten away with a few things, Brooks and Dad worked better with the pressure of adversity. Lehigh had a number of challenges to overcome, and even though they placed in the top ten, they had a better score. Ambler was totally stress free, and their score was far lower. Lehigh also had upward of thirty dogs entered, and Ambler only had twenty-two.

At Princeton, they scored gold. Over forty dogs were entered, and everything from huge crowds to accidents in the ring plagued the competition. If it was adversity they wanted, adversity they got. The ring stewards earned their keep that day.

Four dogs were excused for soiling the ring, and two children broke away from their parents and actually found themselves in the ring where dogs were competing. Two dogs were excused for being overly aggressive, and one mauled the judge with kisses during the stand for examination. None of this bothered our heroes, and they earned a second-place finish and a photograph of them beaming with pride as they received their third and final leg ribbon, making Brooks, CH Jashes Atticus of Ubar CD. CH was for champion from his breed title, and CD was his proudest accomplishment, making him a companion dog.

Three trials and three titles were all they could ask for. Even Mom envied the ease of their accomplishment, since it took five trials to get Shemp's title, and Vanah took six. It was different circumstances though, since she didn't have the coaching Dad did, and she went alone to a number of the trials she participated in. That in itself made it difficult to have any success. But that was all behind them. What direction were they going to go in next? Both were still going to class and training in open obedience, but competing was a distant goal. The winter months were fast approaching, and the distraction of the holidays allowed them to settle down to a more normal routine instead of spending the weekends going to matches and trials.

Chapter 15
Winner, Winner, Turkey Dinner

Brooks loved the holidays, but he never really got the chance to celebrate them when he lived in Maryland. He knew it was a time when people gathered to have a good time and that weeks or months of preparation were devoted to one of the days, culminating in giving and receiving lots of presents. Folks were happy about life and got great joy in wishing one another a Merry Christmas.

Other than what he saw on TV, that about summed up what he knew. Christmas was great, but Thanksgiving was more to his liking. This was a day the family gathered to watch football and eat. *What could be better than that?* A whole day devoted to two things he totally loved: eating and eating. Did I say one of Brooks's favorite things was eating?

In the history of Belgian Tervurens, there wasn't a Terv around who could ever hold a candle to his appetite, nor will there ever be. Amazingly, he was able to stay somewhat slim, weighing in at around seventy-five pounds, normal for a dog his size. Where all that food went was a mystery that the people at Weight Watchers would love to solve; nonetheless, his eating habits were another part of his legend.

Since Thanksgiving is also known as Turkey Day, his eyes grew wide in excitement when he discovered what that was all about. He said, "Bless the Father, bless the Son, and bless the Holy Ghost. He who eats the fastest gets to eat the most." Mashed potatoes and gravy, stuffing and biscuits to go along with all that turkey—just the thought of it made him go wild. Little did he know it wasn't to be. Vanah explained that they might get lucky and find a little extra turkey in their normal ration of Eukanuba lamb and rice and perhaps a little gravy, but other than that, it was whatever they could pick up off the floor after Dad carved the bird.

This was a disturbing turn of events Brooks discovered after confirming it with Pandora who had been there for five holidays.

Dory made food pillaging an art form, having written the "Touch Rule." Pandora discovered during a picnic some years back that humans will not eat anything that was touched first by a dog. Using that philosophy, if there was food within reach, all she had to do was touch it with her nose or tongue. After the customary "ew," nine out of ten times, it became hers to eat. She was the queen of that rule since she was the quietest of the three, often getting her way because she was so subtle.

Brooks became so hyper over the mere mention of food that many times he would go too far and not wait for permission. He just ate what he touched, forcing him into his crate for the duration of the meal.

That first Thanksgiving for Brooks went down in history as an epic event. In the course of human and canine events, when pressured, one can move mountains if the desire is strong enough. In this case, it involved a twenty-four-pound turkey.

It was the Sunday before Thanksgiving Day, and Mom had gone grocery shopping. Dad stayed home and helped out with the cleaning while he glanced at the TV from time to time to watch the Eagles trounce the New York Giants. To be truthful, not much cleaning got done that afternoon, since every time Big Blue got the football, it seemed as if they turned it over to the Eagles, which resulted in a score for the birds. There were high-fives all around for Dad and Brooks.

Vanah and Pandora marveled at how grown men could get so worked up over a game they had no control over. I don't want to make any trouble for the girls, but I think they were both closet Giant fans. Anyway, they were expecting out-of-town guests to stay with them for the week, and the house had to be immaculately clean. That was Dad's job; Mom's job was the cooking.

The menu for the big day was to be a traditional one. Mashed potatoes and gravy, stuffing, green bean casserole, corn, sweet potatoes, and cranberry sauce were all the highlights planned to be on the table along with a homemade pumpkin pie with whipped cream for dessert. Of course, heading it all up would be a huge, succulent butterball turkey to feast on. When Mom came home from the store, Dad helped out with the tons of bags of groceries. Last to come in was the ten-ton frozen Butterball turkey. It actually only weighed twenty-four pounds, but as solid as it was, it might as well have weighed ten tons.

It was late in the afternoon by the time all the groceries had been put away. The late football game started, featuring the stinking Redskins against the lowly Browns. No interest there, and the boys had gotten awfully hungry following the drubbing the Eagles had given to the G-men of New York. Having placed the frozen hulk of a turkey on the kitchen counter, Mom expected it would take at least three days for the big bird to thaw in the refrigerator. She left it out to get a head start.

Feeling the pangs of hunger, Mom suggested that they go out for an early dinner and feed the dogs when they got back. They'd been snacking on Dad's pretzels and chips, so she didn't think they'd be that hungry. The Dublin Diner, where they went most Sunday evenings, was not that far away.

They were only gone for an hour, but the sight that befell them when they got back defied reality. The first thing Dad noticed when he turned on the kitchen light was the empty counter. Why he looked there first was a mystery, but Dad is an anomaly all by himself. Thinking Mom had gone ahead and put the big bird back in the refrigerator, he thought nothing of it—until she asked why he had put the turkey away. They thought someone had stolen it, but whom? At first glance, nothing looked out of place. The house had been clearly locked up when they went out.

As Dad made his way around to the front of the kitchen, his feet suddenly went out from under him. Down he went like a sack of flour. Mom hurried to his side in an attempt to help him and went into a split with both feet sliding out in different directions. She landed on top of Dad.

Stunned by the weird goings on, Dad put his hand to the floor in an attempt to push himself up. His hand was all wet from some slimy substance like the movie *Alien*.

"Look over there," Mom shouted in stunned disbelief. "Isn't that the wrapper to the turkey?"

Gaining his composure, Dad reached out for the discarded plastic. "This sure looks like the wrapping to me. I wonder where—"

He caught a glimpse of what remained of the turkey. The breastbone was all that was left, resting in the middle of the living room floor. Looking around the room, they noticed that Pandora was camped out in the den, oblivious of anything going on.

Vanah was on the couch. When Mom looked at her, Van pointed her nose toward the foyer with an incriminating look. There, standing in the dark, was the sad, pathetic Brooks. His face was totally covered in slime, and he looked as guilty as one could look. Dad thought, *Cats eat canaries, but my dog eats frozen turkeys?*

In the aftermath, the reality was unbelievably true. In less than an hour, Brooks had managed to get a frozen twenty-four-pound turkey down from the counter, which was thirty six inches above the floor, a super feat all by itself. And he managed to devour the big bird in its entirety, leaving only the breastbone as evidence. It was one for the books.

"How can we explain this to anyone?" Dad asked. "Nobody in their right mind would ever believe a dog could consume a whole frozen turkey in less than an hour. A slimy kitchen floor, pieces of plastic wrapping, a breastbone devoid of any meat, and a guilt-riddled dog with gunk all over his face adds up to only one thing!"

"The dog ate the turkey!"

If there was any doubt after that, an hour or so later when the mess was cleaned up and everyone had settled down in the living room to watch some TV, Dad noticed Brooks trotting to the kitchen. Not making anything out of it, he focused back on the show he was watching when he heard a noise come from behind the kitchen table. As he peered around the room, Dad could now render his verdict that Brooks unquestionably ate the turkey.

Despite the setback with the main course, Thanksgiving dinner went off without any major incidents. Mom and Dad's guests arrived and got great pleasure out of seeing how well behaved the three dogs were.

Dad was taken aback by how Brooks never tried to evoke the touch rule at dinner.

Brooks confided in Vanah by telling her that even he thought he had taken the "Turkey Incident," as it came to be known, a little too far, he was going to try to behave for the guests.

As the meal went on, the guests refused to believe the story of the turkey. They tried to be polite and pretended to accept the tale as the absolute truth. After dinner, they retreated to the living room to catch the Cowboys and the Dolphins on the TV.

As Dad and Mom cleaned up in the kitchen, Brooks settled down in the living room to watch the game too. At a commercial, he overheard the man whisper, "Have you ever heard such a tale as they are trying to tell?"

She responded, "You have to be kidding. That dog eating a huge frozen turkey in an hour? I just can't believe it."

The man said, "That dog is only good for playing catch and doing little doggy tricks. He just isn't that smart. I think Jim is blowing the whole thing way out of proportion to make his dog more interesting than he really is."

You don't think dogs understand what people are saying? What happened next might convince you otherwise.

Dad took a little break from drying dishes and stepped in the living room to see how everyone was doing. "What's the score?" Dad asked.

"14–0, Dallas," the man replied. "It's getting interesting and starting to snow. Why don't you leave the dishes and watch?"

Mom replied, "Go ahead. The dishes can wait."

Dad flipped the dishtowel over to the sink and started to make his way over to watch the game.

The woman said, "Can you get us a couple of brews?"

"And get one for yourself too while you're at it," the man added.

Dad thought nothing of it and retreated to the back porch where he had a cooler full of Buds on ice.

Brooks was growing more and more pissed at these phony so-called friends and was waiting for an opportunity to show them that he was a little smarter than they thought. Running out with Dad, an idea popped into his furry head. Poking his nose into the container, he grabbed ahold of a can of beer. Thinking he was being cute, Dad allowed Brooks to carry the can in the house, intending to take it from him before he got too far into the doorway.

As they entered, Brooks took off like a shot and ran up to the man on the couch. With the beer can in his mouth, he proceeded to jump up on him, hind feet on the floor and his front paws squarely on his chest.

The man took it all in stride and got a kick out of the dog bringing him a beer. "Good boy," he said with a laugh. "Give it to me."

Never ever say Brooks disobeyed a command. Clamping down on the can, his big canines ripped several holes and spurted the golden Budweiser all over the man and his wife.

When it was all over, the man and the woman were covered in foamy white beer.

Not smart enough to eat that turkey? Brooks thought, seething inside. I'm smart enough to know I love beer. And if this is the only way I can have some, watch out. My tongue is coming your way!

64

Chapter 16
A Canine Christmas Story

I must say there never was a Thanksgiving that could top the one back in 1993. No way, no how. Brooks was eventually exonerated for his deeds and even the so-called friends were pressed into admitting that he indeed had the ability to eat that turkey. Brooks only regretted that he had to waste a perfectly good can of Budweiser on them to prove it.

All was well in Brookieland, and the Christmas season was soon upon them. Mom was immersed in getting the shopping done since she loved spending Dad's money and was very good at it to boot. Along with his own errands, Dad was responsible for all the outdoor illumination. Leave it to him to come down with dyslexia and put the Noel sign up in the front yard backward. Anyone driving through Blooming Glen couldn't help but get a chuckle out of the beautifully illuminated red-and-green "leoN" sign.

Along with his holiday duties, Dad now had a bizarre new job. It seemed that the folks at the Hilltown Dog Training Club were in need of a secretary, and the president thought Dad might be the best choice for the job. They thought that since he got along so well with everyone, he'd make a good administrator. Convoluted logic for sure, but amazingly, he impressed. First thing he did was design a newsletter that he and the club could be proud of. No more notes and notices typed up on grocery list paper. This was going to be a first-class publication. He got the instructors to write articles, and members now had a special page to brag about their accomplishments. They listed club functions and announcements, and the minutes from the general meetings were recorded so everyone knew what was going on. With all that, he still had time for his signature piece, a fun column he titled "Brooks World."

Brooks World was an article Dad invented in an attempt to poke fun at his lack of dog knowledge and handling skills, told through the eyes of Brooks. Through the crazy antics of Dad and his canine sidekick, people started to loosen up about their inhibitions when it came to their dogs and laughed about their mistakes. Astonishingly enough, it caught on. Dad wound up writing more than thirty-five of these articles over the years.

The first Brooks Word happened to come out several weeks before Christmas.

Dear Santa,

You know me; I'm Brooks, the guy that asked you for the Barcalounger last year. The mat for my crate was nice, but this year, now that I'm in a new home, I would expect your standards to be up to my high expectations. After all, this new family I have adopted is getting my best behavior. About that turkey and beer incident of this past Thanksgiving, isn't it punishment enough that wherever I go, they take up the food and beverages and point at me as if I committed a capital offense; after all, I was exonerated for it.

Enough about me. How are you and the elves doing? I'll bet you have them hopping getting ready for the big day. My sister Pandora should get a little something extra this year for setting me straight about you elves. She explained to me that elves aren't miniature Elvises running around putting on shows to help you defray the costs for all those toys you have to make for everyone. They actually help you do all the work in getting ready for the big day, much like Dad does getting me ready for the dog shows. Come to think of it, Dad kind of has the elf mentality, especially around Mom.

Now that I have all that behind me, I'd like to move on to my list. I kept it modest at least for my standards and feel I'm deserving of everything listed below:

1. *One Barcalounger Reclining Chair (once again, my main request)*
2. *One whole pig on a spit (I got pig ears last year, and they simply won't do)*

3. *One TV remote control with big numbers my paws can operate*
4. *Two or more cases of Budweiser (I trust the Pepto-Bismol I received last year was a joke)*
5. *One Recaro sport bucket seat for the Bronco*
6. *One official Major League Baseball (the tennis balls are for girls)*
7. *Pig ears (come to think of it, they would make nice appetizers)*
8. *A backyard full of that stuff we saw at Timonium last spring—I think they call it agility equipment*

Other than that I think I'll be good to go.
Have a Merry Christmas,
Brooks

Dad now had the ability to get into Brooks's head and write about what was going on, and people loved it. The holiday preparations continued, and the excitement grew for the coming of the big day.

Dad continued to tweak the outside decorations, mainly after getting a spelling lesson from Mom and half a dozen neighbors. Mom continued shopping and planning the guest list for the grand celebration. Christmas always meant a full house.

With Brooks being adopted into the family and all the adjustments to life with three dogs, the human son of Mom and Dad comes to mind. It's not hard to miss a six-foot-three, scrapping dude of twenty lingering around the house. With going to college and working the graveyard shift at the local Mobil service station, Chris usually remained out of sight and mind in the sanctuary of his room—studying, messing around on his computer, or sleeping. He also spent a lot of his time away from home with his friends. Days or weeks could pass, and you'd never know he was around. I'm thinking of him now because over the holidays, he spent more time at home, mostly to keep Mom from killing Dad over anything he'd screw up. I know Vanah wanted to get him a striped referee shirt for Christmas, and Brooks would have liked to give him a whistle to maintain the order.

Chris wasn't much of a domestic animal fan, but he was very good with Brooks. They loved to roughhouse together. Vanah shied away from that sort of thing being the little princess that she was. Pandora could go either way, but mostly she liked to hang out in Chris's room because he had a fish tank. She loved to pass the time by watching them swim around. Chris appreciated the dogs, but he was more into the exotic world of snakes and reptiles. One such critter on his Christmas list was a monitor lizard, and it would remain a wish of his for many years to come.

Christmas meant a full house, and that year was no exception. Mom always invited her mother, sister, and nephew for Christmas Eve, and they usually stayed until the day after. It was a lot of people for such a small house. The chores were endless.

Vanah gave good advice: "Brooks, stay the hell out of the way!"

Mom headed up the operation, assigning work details and making sure they all got done along with the shopping, wrapping, and preparations for the meal.

Chris was in charge of the cleaning, a job he was very good cheating at. Amazing what you could find under cushions and mattresses after he cleaned a room. Dusting was an art form, judging by the creative swirl marks made by his dust rag. All in all, he did a passable job.

Dad would say, "Good enough for government work." Dad had his hands full getting all the decorations up from the basement and putting them out. He had to do it again when Mom decided his way was the— well, let's just say he picked up inside where he left off outside when it came to decoration.

A week before Christmas, Mom and Chris decided to go out and get the bulk of the shopping done. It was an all-day operation. Knowing he would be home with nobody around to interfere, Dad decided to take advantage of the situation and decorated the whole house on his own. One thing about Dad was to not give him time alone to think because you'd regret it every time. The sight that befell Mom and Chris when they got home was nothing shy of incredible.

Upon opening the front door, they were greeted by the melodious sounds of Alvin and the Chipmunks singing about hula-hoops for Christmas and a strong waft of evergreen smacking them in the face.

"Smells like Glade in here," Chris observed. "Did the dogs take a crap?"

As they made their way through the foyer with hands and arms full of parcels from their daylong shopping event, they marveled at Dad's work. Garland laced the banister rail that led up the steps. Trinkets of Santa, snowmen, and elves decorated every space that was available. A string spanned across the top of the French doors that led into the kitchen, and Christmas cards hung from it. A manger scene was spread out on top of the TV, complete with snow on the ground and straw in the cradle. The front corner of the room held the huge balsam tree Mom and Dad had picked out just after Thanksgiving. It was adorned with sparkling bubble lights along with white and colored illuminations, twinkling to the rhythm of the music. Ornaments of all shapes and sizes had been hung on just about every branch, spreading into a perfect conical profile topped with a lighted angel tickling the ceiling.

Mom and Chris stood in amazement, speechless over what a wonderful job Dad had done and how much he had accomplished in such a short time. In past years, it took all three well over a day to accomplish what he had done in a little more than seven hours.

"There's more," Dad proclaimed. "Wait here and don't move." He scurried into the kitchen and around the corner.

A couple of minutes later, Pandora appeared from around the corner. She was sporting a Santa hat and a red coat trimmed in white. He directed her to sit next to the tree while Vanah entered. Vanah wore a red-and-green stocking cap and a red, white, and green plaid vest. She made her way over to sit next to her sister. Neither looked at all happy. They occasionally shook in a vain hope that the garb would mysteriously fall off and disappear.

Dad stood in the doorway calling Brooks, but Brooks decided to go in the other direction. Dad was struggling to keep Vanah and Pandora still and get Brooks to cooperate, so Mom stepped in to help. Trying to keep her composure, she put her packages down and made her way over to the girls to keep them still.

Finally, Dad came across the room with Brooks. "Ta da!" he sang out.

Slowly, Brooks made his way round the corner. Atop his head, he was wearing reindeer antlers with little bells on the ends, tinkling with every humiliating stride.

Dad had rigged up red-and-green lights on his collar that blinked in unison with the vest on his back that had illuminated letters reading "I like Elves" spelled out on both sides. You could see his face glowing red in embarrassment even through all that hair. It was a sight to behold, and Brooks would look to get revenge for it someday. For now, he had to get through the next couple of days before Christmas morning and the rewards that awaited him.

When Chris was a little boy, he started Christmas around four in the morning. He would "accidentally on purpose" make noise in an attempt to awaken his parents and convince them to let him open the many presents left behind by a generous Santa. Dad had a little mean streak about him, and he instructed Santa Claus to make sure the elves wrapped every gift Chris was to receive in order to prolong the suspense of what he might get.

That was then, and this is now. The culprits responsible for an early rise were Vanah, Pandora, and Brooks. Faking that he had to go out, Brooks paced back and forth, making just enough noise to awaken Mom, since an atom bomb couldn't get Dad out of his deep sleep. With Mom awake, the little girl in her would prompt a reveille call, awakening everyone and resulting in the entire family assembling in the living room to begin the grand tradition of opening Christmas presents. The dogs were the first to gather around the tree, sniffing each and every parcel in the hopes that the ones that smelled the best would be theirs.

Brooks was the first one down the steps, and as he stood in the middle of the room, he could hardly believe his eyes. In the far corner was a genuine high-backed Naugahyde Barcalounger, complete with massage, heat controls, and a big red bow. *Virginia, there really is a Santa. The big guy truly came through this time.*

Just as he was going try it out, Mom called the dogs to go out to do their business. Brooks wasted no time in getting his chore done and was back in the house before he could say, "What the heck?" As he hurried into the living room to check out his plush new recliner, Dad was sitting in it and acting as if it were his. Not only that, he was thanking Mom like she had given it to him!

All in all, Christmas was a bust for Brooks, at least according to his Christmas wish list. Even though he conceded the Barcalounger was meant for both Dad and he, he would have preferred sole possession of it. As far as the whole pig on the spit, which was number two on his list, it was pig ears again. He got a remote control in the form of a squeaky toy that Mom thought was adorable. *Adorable won't change the TV controls*, Brookie thought. The Recaro sport bucket seat for the Bronco was just a pipe dream, so no harm, no foul there. No baseball and no Bud, but plenty of stuffed toys and goodies rounded out his haul for the year.

Unbeknownst to Brooks, the last thing on his list would come his way in due time. First, they had to get through the up-and-coming winter. Little did he know that the eighth item on his Christmas list would change his and Dad's life forever. For that matter, it was the catalyst that changed the lives of many others too.

Chapter 17
A New Year, a New Direction

Christmas was now a memory, and Brooks would eventually get over the disappointing results of his wish list. There was always next year, and being a little smarter, his approach would have to take a different tact. For now, the new year meant adventure.

The previous year started out badly but ended about as well as things could get for a two-year-old Belgian Tervuren. He had a new family complete with Mom, Dad, Chris, and two sisters. Dad had helped him get a breed championship and companion dog title to go along with his world record for eating a twenty-four-pound frozen turkey in less than an hour. It was 1994, and things were looking up.

A favorite activity Mom and Dad started to do that year was taking the dogs to Peddlers Village on nice days. It was a quaint place made up of hundreds of unique little shops and restaurants. Its storybook architecture and clay brick walks that intertwined throughout the community made it the perfect place to spend an afternoon browsing and walking a dog.

Brooks loved going there so he could show off and do little tricks that Dad had taught him. It was a big ego trip for him.

Every time Dad walked the dogs in the village, no less than a dozen people would stop to admire them and ask the same questions.

"That's a beautiful dog, what kind is he?"

"He's a Belgian Tervuren."

"A Belgian what?" people would ask. "Where are you from?"

"We're from Blooming Glen," Dad would say.

"Blooming where?"

After a while, it got a little tiresome, but Vanah and Brooks loved how Dad had to keep his composure when approached. It got so annoying that on one occasion a lady came up to the dogs, and before she could even get a word out, Dad said, "Belgian Tervurens, and we're from Blooming Glen!"

Brooks got a real kick out of that incident, but Dad came really close to getting his face slapped. Turns out the woman couldn't have cared less what they were or where they were from, since she was a cat person.

Dad found a remedy to the situation. He had T-shirts printed up so that whenever they were asked those infuriating questions, they'd simply open their coats and point to the front of their shirts: *We're Belgian Whats from Blooming Where!* Problem solved.

For Mom and Dad, the early January days of 1994 were a time of decision. What direction were they going to take with Brooks and Vanah? Dad and Brooks had accomplished their main goal of getting a conformation championship. The companion dog title was just icing on the cake, proving they could do most anything if they worked at it enough. Mom had gotten Vanah's CD title as well and had dabbled in the agility world a little while Dad was doing his obedience trial tour. The decision was difficult for both and for different reasons.

Dad's newsletter was becoming a hit. His boy was giving him plenty of material for his Brooks World feature, and that was making them one of the more popular handling teams in the club. They were not all that great performance-wise, but everyone loved their antics.

The trip to Timonium had gotten him thinking about agility. It was more about the equipment than anything else. Running Brooks in one of those trials would be very cool, but there was money to be made by building and selling that equipment. *Cha-ching, cha-ching,* Dad thought. The dilemma was that Dad thought he owed Hilltown for giving him the opportunity to make something out of Brooks and himself, but this new agility thing fascinated him to no end. Getting involved might just take him away from his responsibilities at the club.

Mom liked working Vanah in the obedience ring, but she felt like Dad and Brooks were overshadowing them. After all, they had been doing it far longer, and when they got their title, little had been made of it. There were no hard feelings or anything like that, but they wanted to carve a niche for themselves and get out of the shadows. After hooking up with a dog agility club in the fall, Mom found they could have some success and their own spotlight. Dad understood totally, and the die was cast.

Their logic was totally sound. Dad and Brooks would continue to do obedience pursuing his CDX title, that's companion dog excellent, while continuing his tenure as club secretary. Mom and Vanah would become more active in dog agility and pursue a possible agility title in the United States Dog Agility Association, USDAA for short. In addition, Dad would satisfy his interest in agility by starting to build the many obstacles Vanah would need to practice at home since the agility club was fifteen miles away. As they slogged through the winter months, they all got a well-deserved rest from the rigors of dog training.

Winter meant snow and ice. For Brooks, it was a phenomenon he had never really experienced. Having lived his early life in Maryland, he never really saw snow. It was not so much that there wasn't any, but his previous owner kept him out of it since she didn't want to be bothered with cleaning him up afterward. It was different now. Mom and Dad loved the snow. They treated it like a holiday for the dogs, letting them out to run in the backyard as long as they could stand it. Afterward, they would pamper them by drying them off with warm towels and feeding them plenty of goodies.

Dad particularly enjoyed standing up on the deck and watching Vanah and Brooks play their patented game of tag in the white stuff. It seemed that his presence made them play even harder. Even in her later years, Pandora loved when it snowed because it was so comforting to her. Watching her try to catch snowflakes with her black tongue put a smile on everyone's face.

Dad kept up with his duties at the club, attending board meetings on the first Monday of each month and a general membership meeting the following Monday. Tuesdays meant class at Hilltown when the weather permitted, and the rest of the time was spent working on the newsletter and his column.

Brooks had gotten into Dad's head. Whenever he sat down to write about his adventures with the dogs, he fell under a spell. He was a chief estimator for the largest electrical contractor in the world, and after reading the many letters and proposals he had written over the years, you'd never think in your wildest dreams he'd be the author of this popular article. It was like they were one—living off each other's personalities and knowing what buttons to push to motivate or irritate one another.

My sister Vanah and I were talking about the two inches of ice we had the other day and how we made Dad come down the hill after us. He used to brag about how he could handle himself on ice, like Wayne Gretzky at a hockey rink, but not that day. I have never seen anyone slide so far on one foot and end up on his head. When he was finished, he had taken out three trashcans and an azalea bush. It took him twenty minutes to get back up that hill! If you heard his side of the story, he had to walk over a hundred yards to get to the house. I think it was fifteen feet, and "walk" was an understatement. It was more like crawling on his belly. What made it worse is that he thought he was saving us by attempting to go down the same hill to get us again. This time, he made the trip on his cedar-rumpus. As we watched him flail like a hooked mackerel, we went over and gave him kisses to make him feel like we cared. Nevertheless, when Mom came to the door and called us for dinner, we kicked it into four-wheel drive and were in the house in a flash, leaving Dad behind in a crumpled heap. When he finally made it to the house, Mom balled him out for playing around and made him take us out front on leashes after our dinner. We won't go into details, but he looked like the Three Stooges on ice, all three. Gosh, I love ice!

After he was finished with getting us inside safely, Mom assumed that he didn't want dinner. She put everything away and retired to the den to watch TV. Knowing she had fixed a nice beef stew for supper, he found a leftover dish of stew in the refrigerator and popped it in the microwave. When it was done, he settled down in the living room in my Barcalounger with his stew and remote control. To Dad, there is nothing better than watching a good college basketball game on TV with a big bowl of Mom's homemade stew. It was just the thing to take the hurt out of his skating adventure. That's what he thought. When Mom came in Dad complimented her on a great meal.

Seeing the leftover dish in the sink, she asked, "You never complimented me before. Why should you now?" Dad remarked, "That's because you never made stew this good in the past."

Mom said, "That's because it's not my recipe. It's Kennel Rations."

In one fell swoop, Dad had managed to piss Mom off by thinking my leftover dinner was her great stew. Don't ask how I felt.

Dad's flair for the dramatic was spot on. Aside from a minor detail or two, I would bet if Brooks could write, that would be the way he'd explain it. Brooks and the girls gave him lots of material to write about over the years, and they did so whenever he had the chance.

By the end of February, the weather had gotten old. Everyone was hoping Punxsutawney Phil would be wrong about seeing his shadow. According to the tradition, if Phil saw his shadow and returned to his hole, he predicted six more weeks of winter. Brooks thought, *Let me at that little bastard. I'll pull that rat out of his hole and make him predict good weather.*

By early March, a few warm snaps started to stir the imagination of getting outside and enjoying their well-laid plans for the future. Dad was itching to get out in the yard and get his garden going, and Mom was anxious to plant her flowers.

During the third week of somewhat calm weather, Mom got a call from the lady at the Keystone Agility Club. They were ready to get the 1994 season started and wanted to know if she was still interested in participating in the club's training program. Mom and Vanah had gone through the beginner's course in the fall, and she didn't have to ask twice if she wanted to continue in more advanced classes.

Though the calendar said it was still winter, the news that Mom was going to start agility classes that Saturday officially made it spring in her book.

Chapter 18
Spring Has Sprung

With the start of agility practice for Mom and Vanah, Dad and Brooks continued with obedience training at Hilltown. They were doing okay, but without Mom and Van to nag them about every little thing, it seemed a little empty.

After a couple of weeks, Dad went to agility class with Mom to take measurements and pictures of the equipment so he could get started on constructing some obstacles for them to practice on at home. At first, this didn't sit well with Brooks, since he always went with Dad when he would go places on the weekend. This was Vanah's gig, and Dad wasn't going to spoil it for her despite the protests.

Brooks even threatened to run away from home, but everyone knew that was a load of bunk since he had to be back in time for dinner. *You get hungry running away.* Instead, he jumped up in the Barcalounger and scratched himself silly, spreading fur all over the seat in protest. Brooks had a temper, and if provoked, he had ways of showing it. To top it off, he ran upstairs, jumped up on the bed, and licked Dad's pillow until it got soaked.

"Have a good night's sleep," Brooks grumbled as he slobbered over the sheets. He didn't know the result of Dad's trip to agility class was the beginning of him getting his last wish on his Christmas list.

Things were much different than Dad had thought at the Keystone Agility Club. Practice was held in an open area behind an antique store. The site was about three acres of lawn and somewhat secluded. However, you didn't want to have an uncontrollable dog running off lead since there was no fencing to keep dogs in or people out. A somewhat heavily traveled county road bordered the far side of the site, which was less than ideal for folks who didn't have a handle on their dogs.

The equipment was stored in an old home-built trailer that had seen its better days ten years earlier. Mom introduced Dad to the equipment manager, and they hit if off right from the start. All you had to do was show Dad a screwdriver to get his attention for life. It didn't hurt that she—yes, the equipment manager for the Keystone Agility Club was a lady—knew little to nothing about the construction of the obstacles. Karen had gotten the job because she liked to paint. Dad loved the construction; like peanut butter and chocolate, they became a perfect match. They were the Reese's Peanut Butter Cups of agility equipment. It wasn't his intent to get involved in the club, since he already had his hands full up at Hilltown, but when he saw the sad state of the obstacles, he couldn't refuse their plea for help. To this day, Dad believes he was set up.

While Mom and Vanah worked out on the equipment, Dad took copious notes. He snapped pictures and made measurements of each and every item. Once he was done, he asked if he could borrow a couple of jumps to use as guides to replicate his own.

Karen obliged under the condition that he would take the two that needed repair and fix them. It's no wonder how Dad got one of his many nicknames. They called him "Stradivarius" because they could play him like a violin.

Dad felt badly that Brooks was left behind. He also borrowed a tunnel, thinking he would make it up to Brooks by playing with him when he got home.

Upon entering the house, Dad called for Brooks to come outside to see what he had for him. Normally he would fly down the steps, boiling over with excitement to see what Dad had brought, but this was different. He was upset and didn't know what was going on.

As Brooks slowly made his way to the door, he saw Dad out in the yard, calling for him to try out this crazy new thing called a tunnel. He was stunned. Dad didn't forget his boy after all. For once in his life, Brooks was so excited he couldn't move, although his tail was going at a hundred miles per hour.

"Come on, buddy. Check it out!" Dad yelled.

Brooks jumped off the top step of the deck, eight feet off the ground, and hit the ground at full stride. He bowled over Dad, mauling him with kisses and hugs. All was forgiven.

When Dad finally recovered from all the affection thrown at him by his boy, he was amazed by how he knew to run in the one end of the flexible tube and dart out the other. He'd never done this obstacle before, but he knew just what to do. They ran around the yard like madmen, always ending up at one end of the tunnel or the other, thrilling Dad with his performance.

The day had been long but very productive. Dad was the unofficial equipment manager for Keystone Agility, a position he insisted he was set up for.

Mom said, "Old Stradivarius Loveless could never turn down anything that involved power tools."

Mom and Vanah were happy in their new world of agility, building confidence and improving with every practice.

Brooks was having fun with the equipment Dad was bringing home.

Dad decided to call it a night early since he had lots to do in the morning. As he got ready, he noticed the bed had been roughed up a little. He thought nothing of it. It wasn't unusual for any one of the dogs to hop up and take a nap when left alone during the day. Dad climbed in and was out like a light seconds after his head hit the pillow.

At about midnight, just as he was to embrace the bodacious Bo Derek who was running toward him on the beach with open arms, Dad was awakened with a soggy pillow to the head.

In appreciation for bringing home the tunnel, Brooks had managed to swap pillows with Mom to show Dad he really wasn't mad at him for leaving him behind.

Mom mumbled, "You'd better tell your son not to forget who feeds him."

With that said, it was back to the beach for Dad.

Chapter 19
Change Can Be Good

A somewhat dry spring turned into a very hot summer. Mom and Vanah did dog agility, and Dad and Brooks stuck with obedience. Dad's garden did very well early in the season with a very nice strawberry yield. Unfortunately, he only got half a crop, since Vanah ate the rest.

Brooks got the blame, but logic prevailed and implicated Little Miss Prissy with the crime. What did her in was that each strawberry only had a small bite taken out, just below the stem, and leaving the top of the berry on the vine. If Brooks had been the culprit, there would be nothing left. Case closed! For a change, the blame went to someone other than Brooks. Also, he had his heart set on a much bigger prize—the watermelon.

As well as things seemed to be going with Vanah and Brooks that summer, Pandora was having her troubles. She had always been content to stay out of the limelight and live out her years resting comfortably in the den or watching the fish in Chris's room. Recently, Brooks noticed that she was spending all her time in the den and had gotten a bit grumpy.

Dad told Brooks that she was grouchy because she was sick. Why her? She seemed like a good little girl, but he had never taken the time to really get to know her.

Dad said, "Life isn't fair sometimes, and we have to live with the hand that's dealt us."

One afternoon when he was sleeping in his Barcalounger, Brooks opened his eyes and Pandora was staring him in the face. As he reared back, she licked his paw, turned, and slowly made her way back to her room. He never saw her again. He was told she had a serious eye problem

79

and couldn't go on any longer. Later that summer, he found himself in her room. It had been several months since Pandora left them, and he still felt her presence. Looking around where she used to stay, Brooks thought about how he would have felt if he had really gotten to know her. Life went on, and Vanah had a new place in his heart.

It took awhile to get over losing Pandora, but as the summer months pressed into the fall, the garden, flowerbeds, and dog training gave them strength to put her loss behind them.

Mom and Dad were slowly drifting away from the obedience world. Dad spent most of his spare time during the summer building agility equipment, and short of tunnels and other items he couldn't make, he now had what turned out to be a full course of obstacles. His work was so good that he sold a few jumps to members of the agility club as well.

Brooks had become Dad's quality control specialist and tested every piece that was made. They still trained every Tuesday night, but Dad's heart just wasn't in it compared to the previous summer.

Mom devoted all of her time to running Vanah in agility. Now a full-fledged member of the Keystone Agility Club, the only time she spent with Hilltown was the occasional meeting with Dad or working as a ring steward at the annual obedience match. Other than that, Vanah's life was devoted to agility.

Dad made it a point not to take Brooks to any of Mom's agility functions. He didn't even take him when he went to work on the equipment and knew no one would be there. This was Vanah's world, and that was that.

At home, it was a different story. Brooks worked on the equipment with Dad, making sure everything checked out. When his sister was practicing, they stayed away. It all balanced out, and when October rolled around, it was trial time for Vanah.

Mom chalked up Vanah's first agility trial as a very good learning experience to say the very least.

Dad thought it sounded like the operation was a success, but the patient died.

In the standard course, she had to run a course that was made up of eighteen basic obstacles. She completed the run and had no faults, but she was way over time. The second event was a jumper's course that consisted of sixteen various jumps and two tunnels. Again, she was a little slow and knocked down a bar. She didn't qualify in that event either. The only discouraging thing that came out of her runs was her speed, and that was essential if she was going to qualify and compete for a placement ribbon.

Since it was a two-day event and Vanah was entered in another standard run, Mom asked Dad if he would be willing to come out and observe. Even though he was not up on all the nuances of handling a dog in agility, he knew enough to be objective.

Mom had learned to trust his opinions when it came to working with the dogs. They had left Brooks at home, but Chris was willing to take care of him so the pillows stayed dry.

At the trial, Dad played it smart. Before Vanah ran, he observed how the other handlers worked their dogs to get familiar with the routine and protocol of agility. It wasn't that far removed from obedience as far as keeping the dog focused on the commands. In fact, he could tell the difference between the teams that had formal obedience training and those that didn't. The ones that did were far, far better. After sharing his findings with Mom, he found a spot where he could observe Vanah's run undetected and also get a few action shots with the camera.

By the time Mom and Vanah ran their run, the coolness of the early morning had translated to warm and sticky, unusual for mid-October in southeast Pennsylvania. Dad's nerves were tense as they ran in the hopes that they could get it together and qualify.

From the very first obstacle, it was evident that today wasn't their day. It took over ten seconds to get Van over the first jump, and with a qualifying score of fifty-two, the seconds became scarcer and scarcer to come by. No matter what Mom did or how much encouragement she tried to give, Vanah had no pep. Instead of running, she approached each obstacle in a trot or walk, hesitated, and then did what was required to get over it before looking for direction.

Mom got more exercise flailing her arms and running back and forth than Vanah did. In the end, the results were the same as the day before— no faults and a nonqualifying time. Dad knew a consoling hug for both was all that he could do, but that really didn't help much.

Disappointed, they packed their things and made their way home.

Mom didn't have to be a genius to know their failed attempt at competing in agility had a lot to be desired.

Vanah needed something to motivate her. She ran fine in practice, but she was a different dog at the trial. Dad observed that when they were at practice, it was usually in the evening and much cooler. Furthermore, there weren't as many distractions. At the trial, there was a lot of activity outside the ring.

This agility sport was turning out to be a lot harder than it looked, at least when it came to competing. With one trial under their belts and the season winding down, Vanah's problems were all too clear—but how to solve them wasn't. The good news was that they had all winter to work it out.

In the early nineties, dog agility wasn't that popular. Trials and matches were not found during the winter months in the Northeast, and most folks worked on obedience or took the time off. Since Dad had built most of the obstacles for a basic course, they practiced when the weather permitted.

With Vanah devoted entirely to doing agility, Dad and Brooks still worked on their obedience. It was hard for the two of them; the more they watched Van train, the more they wanted to get involved. Dad had to remind them that this was Vanah's show.

When Mom took Vanah out back to work on the equipment, Brookie would get up on the sofa and stare endlessly out the window. He made high-pitched whimpers in the hopes that someone would let him out to play. It just wasn't meant to be. It was going to be a long winter, and there was nothing they could do about it.

Thanksgiving had come and gone, and it was uneventful. The turkey antics from the past year had everyone on guard, and the day passed with no food-related incidents.

Dad had the day after off and chilled with Brooks while Mom took Vanah out to practice.

As the door closed behind them, Brooks didn't take his usual position on the sofa to watch. Instead, he jumped in Dad's lap as he tried to read the sports page. Making a general pest of himself, he nagged Dad to the point that he had no choice but to take him out, thinking he had to do his business.

Dad went out the door first to warn Mom that Brooks needed to come out, but before he could take a step, Brooks shoved his way past and literally leaped from the second step of the deck to the ground and proceeded to disrupt Mom's activities.

First Brooks dive-bombed Vanah, nipping her in the rear end as he flew by. Next, he launched himself onto the A-frame, leaping over the peak in a single bound and landing on the ground on his front paws. His rear legs caught up and propelled him to a set of jumps. He leaped up and flew to the next jump. In no particular order, he managed to work himself over every obstacle at least twice.

Dad was able to slow him down by baiting him with a piece of hot dog Mom had given him to help slow his untimely exhibition.

"What the heck was that all about?" Mom said.

Dad said, "I thought he needed to go out to do his business. I guess he had other thoughts."

Vanah slipped out of Mom's grip and flew by Brooks, nipping him in the butt as she flew by. She made a beeline through the tunnel, stopping at the other end to see if her brother was in pursuit.

Dad, holding on to his boy with everything he had, finally let loose at Mom's request.

"What the hell?" she exclaimed. "Let them have their fun."

Brooks sprinted to the tunnel entrance where his sister had been standing as she made a U-turn out the other end. When Brooks tore out, he expected to see Vanah, but she eluded him by entering the other end of the tunnel. When she exited, she started chasing him.

For a solid ten minutes, Mom and Dad were mesmerized by the games they were playing, faking each other in and out of tunnels and over jumps.

"If Vanah could only run that way in a trial," Mom said.

"Now that's the Vanah that needs to show up at the trials."

When the two dogs finally tired, they came up to the house to get a drink of water and rejuvenate themselves.

Mom made her way back to the agility equipment and stared at the obstacles.

Dad sensed something was wrong. "Why the gloomy look? Something the matter?"

Mom turned and said, "Brooks should be doing this. He's a natural at it."

"No," Dad exclaimed. "I agreed to let this sport be for you and Vanah. We have our obedience to work on."

Mom walked over to the A-frame and leaned up against it. "You and Brooks could be so good at this. There is no reason why we both couldn't compete."

Dad wasn't going to admit it—at least not to Mom—but those were the very words he was hoping to hear. He knew very well that this sport was made for them, but he didn't want to horn in on their fun. He'd had a feeling they'd get their chance in time.

"Are you sure? I mean there isn't any reason why we can't team up and do this together. But you have to be okay with it."

Mom looked Dad square in the eye and said, "Didn't you see how Brookie motivated Van just now? That was a sign to tell us that we are a team. With both of us working together, we can't fail."

Dad turned and looked at Vanah and Brooks by their water dishes. "So it be written; so it be done. We're in!"

Their lives would change forever. Dog agility would rule their lives from that point on.

Chapter 20
I Pronounce You
an Agility Dog

In early spring, Dad and Brooks started their orientation to dog agility. There were no formal classes at Keystone since they really didn't have an established training program.

Several members who had started the club in 1987 and had been competing for several years took it upon themselves to do an introduction with new members and get them started in the basics. After that, you were on your own more or less to train at your own pace. Classes, if you want to call them that, consisted of a group of members setting up the equipment, usually a course they had run in a past trial. Two or three people would act as spotters to help the beginners through obstacles they were having trouble with and would give them some basic handling techniques. The beginners would have an hour before the advanced folks would show up to do their work. Usually a dog and handler would be evaluated in six weeks, and if they could do the obstacles off lead, then they were allowed to train with the more advanced group.

Brooks's orientation was handled by Alana, "The Lean Mean Agility Machine" as she was known. She was the founder and president of the club and also a judge. She was the best in the club, having several advanced titles under her belt. Dad couldn't have gotten a better mentor. Though Brooks was a fast learner, Dad needed someone with lots of patience to get him through the initial stages, and Alana was just that person.

Alana and Dad knew one another from his dealings with her as the club's unofficial equipment manager. Brooks had never met her, and with all the dealings she had with dogs in agility, she had never encountered a Tervuren. Standard poodles were her forte, and she handled one of the top poodles in agility.

When Dad showed up for his lesson, everything had already been set up. All that needed to be done was introducing Brooks to Alana. Whenever Dad introduced his boy to someone new, he gave them several treats so they could get on his good side.

As Alana approached with cookies in hand, they thought they witnessed trumpets playing in the background and the clouds parting in the heavens as Brooks ignored the handout. He stood in silent awe, admiring all the agility equipment that stood majestically before him. He slowly walked past his instructor who had knelt down in front of him and was holding her hand out with the goodies. When he reached the end of the lead, it grew tight; with that, he started to quiver with excitement. Turning his head back at Dad, he thought, *Let's get this show on the road.* In all of history, it was the first time he had turned down food for anything. It was an amazing spectacle.

Having gotten over what Dad has often called, "The Immaculate Introduction," it was time to get to work. Alana proceeded to introduce the first group of obstacles, which were the jumps. In the early nineties, USDAA was by far the most popular agility organization, and Keystone adopted their standards.

For Brooks's height, he would be jumping a thirty-inch bar. For now, the bar was set at eighteen inches, mainly to get him going. Dad lined him up, and he went over it just like he was in his backyard. Again, they lined up to go back the other way, and again, nothing to it.

Alana warned Dad to resist the temptation of raising the bar too soon in his early learning stages. She told Dad to get Brooks's hips checked by a vet.

"Nothing worse for a dog with bad hips than to be jumping," she said.

When they moved on to the tunnels and chute, they got through them with ease. Brooks had a lot of experience working with those obstacles while playing with Vanah in their yard. The pause table was easy since it was like jumping up on the bed. When he tried it for the first time, his aggressive, hard-charging approach caused him to slide off the back. He landed on the ground on all fours.

Dad said, "You need to use your brakes a little better when you're on that thing."

Alana only sighed and had them do it again.

The second time was much better. When Brooks approached the table, he stopped and hopped up, allowing him to stay planted there. She explained that the table, even though it was set at an eighteen-inch height, would be like the jumps at thirty inches when he was ready.

Like everything else, they did each exercise three times. Despite Dad's unorthodox handling technique, Brooks did exceptionally well.

"Your dog is a natural at this," Alana marveled. "When you get your handling technique down, I think you might have some titles in your future."

Dad beamed with pride.

Now that the easy stuff was behind them, up came the dog walk, A-frame, and teeter-totter. These strange-looking structures would be the single group of obstacles that menaced Brooks and Dad throughout their agility careers.

The A-frame was an imposing edifice, which was sixty inches tall at its peak. It was thirty-six inches wide, and each side was nine feet long. For introduction and training, the height was set at thirty-six inches.

When Dad lined Brooks up for his initial run, he took off like he had been shot from a cannon and bounded over it like it was a steeple jump.

"Whoa, guys!" Alana shouted. "Not good!" Bringing them back for their second go-around, she sat them down and said, "With a fast dog like Brooks, you have to approach these obstacles slower and in control."

"Slow" and "control" were two foreign words to Dad when it came to handling Brooks in agility. As they listened to Alana's tutelage, two more words crept into their vocabulary that were even harder to grasp. "Contact zones" were yellow areas painted thirty-six inches at the bottom of each panel to control the dog's entry and exit. These "horror zones," as Dad used to describe them, were also painted on the dog walk and the teeter-totter.

Alana explained that these areas were commonly known as safety zones. "An out of control dog on a contact obstacle could be very dangerous," she explained. "Let's do it again and slower."

Their next attempt netted a similar result. Though Brooks didn't hurdle the top like he had the first time, he jumped over the yellow like it was something to avoid. Even after Alana had Brooks start from a sit and two feet from the front, he still managed to launch himself over the contact zone on his approach.

Dad managed to slow him down on his exit, and he had a successful completion.

"You have your work cut out for you," she observed. "I can't stress working on these obstacles more, and if you don't, they could be your downfall. We could work on this all day, but we have other things to accomplish. Let's move on."

The dog walk resulted in a little better performance, but Brooks's eagerness to get on and off the obstacles was making him hard to control even though he was being handled on lead throughout the lesson.

With each pass Brooks and Dad made, Alana took notes, more so than any other potential student she had ever indoctrinated into the sport. They were making quite an impression—both good and bad.

As for the teeter-totter, Alana had to be extra careful not to spook the dog, since this was the only moving obstacle. With a bad experience there, it could take forever to undo the damage. She wasn't worried though, since Brooks appeared to be one of those fearless dogs that could overcome most anything thrown at him, but she took every precaution to ensure success.

They slowly approached the obstacle with Alana on Brooks's left and Dad on his right. As they reached the section where the plank would pivot, Alana instructed Dad to stop Brooks and hold him while she pushed down on the board so the end was now on the ground. They stood there for a couple of seconds so they could get acclimated to the movement of the obstacle. Once she was sure Brooks wasn't going to jump off like a lot of dogs would do at that critical point, he was allowed to proceed slowly down and off, making sure contact was made on the yellow.

"That was very well done," she said. "Let's do it again."

The second try was even better than the first. Brooks anticipated the movement of the plank and stopped on his own when Alana pushed it to the ground. A nice exit resulted with his paws making contact in the yellow and more praise. Amazed by the success, she allowed Dad to handle Brooks by himself and stood by to keep him from falling. Even though he was on lead, you would have thought he had done this obstacle before. The teeter-totter was the only contact obstacle he hadn't done—even though Dad had built one for their backyard—but Alana was very impressed.

With another student waiting in the wings, time had run out. The hour was just about up, and it didn't look like they'd get the last obstacle in. Fortunately, Karen was responsible for the next lesson. Having never seen Brooks before, she was anxious to see what he could do. She agreed to let them continue the lesson and learn what it took to do the elusive weave poles.

The weave poles were the most difficult objects to learn and could take many months to just be able to get through all twelve without help. Some dogs never learned them well, and they would be the number-one obstacle to losing time during competitions. They consisted of twelve posts, thirty-six inches long, set vertically in a row and spaced eighteen inches apart. The dog had to enter them on the right and weave in and out the entire length of the row without missing a single one. The bigger the dog, the harder it was since the spacing was more difficult for a large dog to get through than a small one.

The poles were set at angles to form a V. At first, Brooks would run through the middle of the V to get used to the poles. He did this with ease. After several successful passes, the poles were raised slightly to narrow the V, forcing him to weave just a little, but that was as far as they went in the initiation stage. Training on this object would take lots of time and tons of patience to get the poles to the full vertical position in which he would be weaving. Dad had time and patience, and this would become Brooks's signature obstacle. For the time being, it was a work in progress.

Alana's report card on Brooks and Dad was summed up in these words: *Brooks has the speed and quickness needed to become an excellent agility dog. He is fearless and hard charging; however, these qualities have to be harnessed if he is to be successful. His handler has the physical capabilities to run with Brooks but needs to focus on where he wants his dog to go when running a course and set a vocabulary for his dog to understand. Work on the contact obstacles, especially the A-frame, is a must. I hereby recommend them to beginners' agility and proclaim Brooks an agility dog.*

Chapter 21
That Was Then, This Is Now

Dad was stoked when he and Brooks got home from the orientation lesson with Alana. The first thing he did was take inventory of what obstacles they had and what he needed to build to take this agility thing to a higher level. The sport was relatively unknown, and the equipment was hard to find and very expensive.

If you were creative and had some carpentry experience, most of the items could be made fairly easily without breaking the bank. If you knew anything about Dad, it was that he hated to buy anything he knew he could build himself. When the inventory was done, which took all of about a minute and a half, he had his work cut out for him. They had an A-frame, a dog walk, and a teeter-totter. The contact items were covered, and only three jumps and a makeshift table summed up the rest. If Mom and Dad were really serious about their involvement in agility, time and money would have to be invested in making more obstacles.

For now though, they had to make do with what they had, since time was becoming an issue for Dad. With working all day at his real job, he rarely got home before six in the evening. With dinner and the occasional chore or two, he was lucky to be free by seven thirty at the earliest to train with Brooks or build any new equipment they needed to complete their wish list.

To further complicate things, Dad was still secretary at Hilltown. Two nights per month were devoted to meetings, recording the minutes, and writing the newsletter. Brooks World had become a hit, and lord forbid if the Hilltown Howler was published without its monthly account of the life and times of its clown prince of Tervs. Tuesday night obedience class and Thursday night beginner's agility took up any spare time he had.

The weekends were filled with things that needed to be done around the house, like mowing, house repairs, and improvements. The garden was being neglected more and more.

Thursday night beginner's agility was fast becoming the highlight of the week for Brooks and Dad. Since where they trained was halfway between work and home, Dad would go to the site from work and meet Mom there with Brooks. After the first couple of weeks—and quickly absorbing all that was being taught—Dad started to show up earlier and earlier to help with setting up. The more time with the equipment and people with experience setting it up gave him the ability to duplicate similar exercises and courses at home.

The more Dad got involved, the better he and Brooks got, and it was rubbing off on Mom and Vanah as well. Practice was making perfect, and the marked improvement over last year was evident. Both dogs complemented each other's training, even though Vanah was competing and Brooks was only a beginner. They worked great together. Mom would run Van over an obstacle, and Dad would follow with Brookie, duplicating his sister's every move like they were playing Simon Says.

Unlike the other dog activities, agility was far more complex to train for. From mastering the equipment to handling the obstacles in a course, it wasn't something you just went out and did. It took lots of work and experience. Because of all that had to be learned, the summer would be full of decisions and challenges. Agility filled up all their spare time.

By the end of spring, Dad was rarely attending obedience classes. In fact, he missed every class in June. Much worse than that, he had to find a substitute to take the minutes for the board meetings. He missed two of the last four. The newsletter was suffering as well, and as far as his fabled Brooks World, the last two he managed to scroll out were devoted to his agility activities—not what the obedience crowd was really interested in reading about.

Something had to give. Agility had become a higher priority than obedience, and Dad felt badly about that. He believed he owed a lot to Hilltown since they were the ones who had put him on the map, but Mom soberly reminded him that his position as secretary wasn't handed to him because of his qualifications. It was more that no one else could be suckered into it.

Dad's head was so swollen over them asking him to be a member of the board that he was unaware that he was their fifth choice. He also lost sight of the fact that he had been duped into the position, which actually turned him into a fairly decent secretary, at least until now.

On the eve of Hilltown's annual picnic, the president of the club called Dad and asked for his resignation. They needed someone to be at all the meetings and carry on the business of the organization—and that wasn't being done. Dad had raised the standards of his position from when he took over and could no longer keep up with them.

At the picnic, it was announced that Dad was resigning his position as secretary. An appreciative board of directors issued a proclamation of appreciation for all he had done. Everyone in attendance rose to give him a standing ovation, and he became a regular member. Dad was free to give dog agility his full effort, but he missed the mystique of being a board member, since it had given him clout in his own mind.

Dad continued to go to obedience on Tuesdays, but the urge to complete the agility equipment inventory drew them away for good after about three weeks. They really weren't getting anything out of the training since he had resigned himself to the fact they weren't going to pursue any future titles. Obedience titles were then; agility titles were now.

Chapter 22
The Plain, Ugly Truth

Now that Mom and Dad were totally focused on dog agility full time, it was time to do some serious planning for the future. Mom entered Vanah in a number of trials that summer, and Dad's goal for Brooks was to enter him in Keystone's joint trial with the Baltimore group late in October. It would be their first attempt in competing, and as the summer pressed on, big things were expected for Team Brooks.

Brooks graduated from beginner's status with exceptional potential. Individually, he could perform each obstacle as good as or even better than the most experienced dogs in the club, including Alana's champion poodle. However, when stringing them together in a sequence or running a course, Brooks's hard-charging passion caused him to down jump bars, stray off course, and miss contact points. He was two dogs in one; the first was calm and collected doing one obstacle at a time, but the wild man would come out when he did two or more at a time. All kinds of drills and exercises were tried, and they occasionally had success, but the contacts were always the killer. Yellow was fast becoming a color neither Brooks nor Dad liked.

In all the confusion of training tips and suggestions for how to calm Brooks down, one of Dad's running mates asked Dad if Brooks was still intact. It was her opinion that male dogs were easier to handle after they had an operation to calm them down, better known as neutering.

After deliberating with Mom, they decided to take the matter up with an expert. They went to the doctor to see what he thought. Dr. Lovis Mev was Brooks's vet. He was a dark, mysterious gentleman in his late sixties with the appearance of an undertaker.

93

You never saw him entering or exiting a room; he just appeared or disappeared like a ghost in a haunted house. Dad's first impression was that he resembled Gomez Adams in a lab coat, complete with beady eyes, dark mustache, and pinstripe pants. He even sported a long Cuban cigar when he was off duty. When the doctor talked, he had a tendency to draw out every O and E, making his conversations sound like sermons.

"Hello. Please sit down," Dr. Mev said.

If he didn't take notes or have his assistants write things down for him, he would hardly remember anything. But that was all a façade. The doctor had a tremendous gift for treating animals, and though he came off as eccentric to people, pets loved him. Brooks was one of only a handful of dogs the good doctor was willing to get close to. Vanah thought the turkey incident had impressed Dr. Mev so much that he actually wrote about it in a medical journal he published. What some dogs will do for attention, she would say.

The doctor agreed neutering could help take the edge off a high-strung dog and recommended it in this case. Unless they were going to breed him, there was no need for him to stay intact. That wasn't what Brooks wanted to hear and could account for him humping the doctor's female assistant when the appointment was over. While they were at it, Dad asked the doctor's opinion about getting his hips checked. He strongly believed all dogs should have their hips graded to ensure a healthy future. In the case, it was especially important since they were competing in agility.

Dr. Mev would do the neutering operation in his office, but the hip evaluation had to be done at a clinic that specialized in animal orthopedics. It was decided to get his hips taken care of first, since the clinic where the procedure had to be done had an opening the next day. If they didn't take it, they would have a two-month wait until the next opening. With the appointment scheduled for a Tuesday morning, Mom wound up taking Brooks since Dad couldn't get off work that day.

Brooks got through the examination okay, but when Dad got home, he could tell his boy had gone through the wringer. To obtain the X-rays, it was important that he be completely relaxed. For his comfort and safety, it required sedation because the various positions needed for the X-rays would be too painful if he were not. Three separate radiographs were made to show how his hip was oriented in the socket. Hip dysplasia, defined as "an abnormal formation of the hip socket that, in its more

94

severe form, can eventually cause crippling lameness and painful arthritis of the joints," was the main thing that was looked for. So even though Brooks was out for the procedure, when he came to, he could feel the affects of the different poses he had been forced into.

It was an effort to roll his eyes in an attempt to see if anyone was in the room. He made no effort to move.

Dad had never seen him so quiet and subdued. "Is it normal for him to be this wiped out from getting his hips checked?"

"Most of what he's going through is grogginess from the sedation," Mom responded. "Leave him be for a now. When he gets hungry, he'll be back to normal."

Brooks was left to himself while everyone else went about his or her business. It was strange eating dinner and not having two dogs searching for dropped scraps of food. Vanah was in heaven; she took advantage of double the crumbs since Dad was particularly messy that night.

Brooks slept his misery away. It wasn't until the middle of watching *Home Improvement* that Brooks had made his way over to the Barcalounger and put his head on Dad's lap. Sensing he may be a bit hungry, he was given his dinner. Nibbling at it at first, Brooks's appetite got the best of him.

"Looks like you're back," Dad said with a laugh before letting him out to do his business.

Brooks slowly made his way down the steps and still felt a little stiff, but by the time he had finished doing what he needed to do, he was acting more like his old self again.

Back in the house, Dad knelt down and gave his boy a big hug and assured him that everything would be okay. As they sat on the kitchen floor together, Dad would take the tip of Brooks's ear and massage it with his thumb and middle finger. It was something someone at Hilltown had taught him to do to calm him down before going into the ring, and it grew into a way that Brooks knew that Dad was there for him. It was times like these that made Dad realize that their bond together was growing stronger all the time.

By the next day, Brooks had gotten over all the effects and was his old, hungry hard-charging self again. When let outside to play, he cornered Vanah and said, "Yesterday didn't happen."

They went off to play one of their patented games of tag. Even though what Brooks had endured wasn't any big deal, Dad played it safe and didn't do any agility that day. They attended class the following day, and Brooks was back, missing contacts and driving his dad crazy in his quest to slow him down.

About a week later, Dad got a call from Mom at work.

"Dr. Mev's office called and wants to meet with us to discuss the results of the hip evaluation," she said.

"Is everything okay?" he asked.

"They wouldn't say, just that the doctor wants us there with Brooks. Everything could be all right, but the fact that they won't say has me worried. I told them we'd be there tonight. Get home as soon as you can."

The rest of the day dragged while Dad wondered what to expect. When Vanah had her hips checked, they had called Mom and given her the results over the phone. Even way back when they had Shemp, they called about his major hip problems. *Why the mystery?* He kept saying it was just the way Dr. Mev was, since the vet had a flair for the dramatic.

Dad made it home, picked everyone up, and got to the doctor's office well before the appointment time in an attempt to weed something out of the receptionist. She was as tight lipped as a zipper. When they were escorted into the examination room, Dr. Mev appeared out of nowhere and said, "Hello. Please sit down."

Here we go, Dad thought. *Another sermon.*

Mom thought the same thing, sat back, and prepared herself for what was to come.

The doctor sat on his swivel stool and rolled up to Brooks. He handed him a goody and pushed back against the wall. Looking up at Dad and seeing he had no treats, Brooks made his way over to the doctor, sat in front of him, and gave him his paw.

"Very smart puppy you are," he said. Massaging the dog's head and settling in for a long talk, he continued, "You people know I don't get personal with my patients. If I did, I wouldn't last very long in this business. So many times, I have bad news to convey. Even though I feel I'm pretty successful in helping the animals get through their problems, I can't afford to get too close to them if I can't cure them." Looking down at Brooks, he vigorously rubbed his head and went on. "There are exceptions to every rule, and your young Terv is one of those exceptions. Ever since you've been bringing this fine boy to me, I have grown very fond of him. You might say he's become one of my favorites. I guess I can afford this luxury every so often as long as I don't make it a habit."

Dad looked at Mom with a puzzled expression and then back to the doctor. "What are you getting at, Doctor?"

"Sounds like we're in for some bad news," Mom responded, clasping Dad's hand to brace herself for the response.

"Well," the doctor explained, "it's a good news–bad news type of thing we have here. The good news is that he doesn't have dysplasia."

Mom breathed a huge sigh, remembering what they had gone through with Shemp.

"So what's the bad news?" Dad asked.

Reaching into his pocket and giving Brooks another treat, the doctor sat straight in his chair. "When dogs' hips are evaluated, they are graded excellent, good, fair, or poor. In your dog's case, he rates only fair."

Dad fell back in his seat and took a few seconds to comprehend. "And that means what?"

Dr. Mev said, "Let's just say it's not the end of the world. In Brooks's formative years, how was he treated?"

Mom said, "Well, we adopted him when he was a little more than a year old, so we don't know that much. His original owner had him mainly for breed competition."

The doctor said, "I mean, what were his living conditions? Did he get plenty of exercise? Was his diet good? Can you tell me anything about that?"

Dad straightened up in his chair and slapped both hands down on his knees. "I don't believe he had the best of care. His diet was probably okay, but from what little I know, he was low man on the totem pole where he came from."

"Please go on," the doctor said. "How was he low man on the totem pole?"

Dad started to get excited. "The gal that had Brooks before we got him raised basenjis. Why she wanted a Terv is anybody's guess. She wasn't equipped to handle a dog like Brooks! He seemed to be treated like he was an outsider, and I don't believe he ever got a whole lot of exercise in her small yard. It appeared that he was kept in a crate most all the time he was inside and was only let out for exercise a few times a day." Dad was getting hot and continued his rant. "When we first got Brooks, I always had the feeling that he thought we were his liberators. He couldn't wait to get out of that house! I don't think he was ever abused physically, but there is such a thing as mental abuse."

Mom pressed forward from her relaxed pose and said, "I never knew you thought that way about where he came from."

"Well, I'm not exaggerating, am I?" he asked.

"Doctor, I'm afraid my husband is dead on," Mom added. "I guess we gave his former owner a lot of credit due to the success she had with him in the breed ring. It took a lot for her to give him up, and we gave her a lot of respect for that."

The air was clear now. A lot of emotion came out of the doctor's simple question.

"I'm not going to sugarcoat the bad news, though like I said before, it's not the end of the world," the doctor explained. "From what I can tell, his hips are only rated fair because during those early months as he grew, he wasn't given the proper exercise to allow his joints to form correctly. Being kept in a crate the majority of the time caused his hips to improperly seat. For now, he is okay, and there is nothing we need to do except give him a normal life."

Dad looked at Mom and back at the doctor. "What do you mean by for now?"

The doctor suddenly got serious. "I believe Brooks has five good years in him to do all the things a normal Tervuren can and wants to do. After that, you'll have to take it easy with him, since he will start to develop an arthritic condition within those hip joints that will eventually cause him great pain. His right hip is where you'll notice him having the most problems since that hip seems to be the worst." He leaned forward and started to scrunch Brooks's ears. "Right now, you have a very normal Terv that is in excellent health, and you should continue to do the things you're doing. There is no reason this boy can't live a normal, healthy life."

Dad said, "I noticed you left out 'long.'"

Dr. Mev smiled and said, "That's up to someone else on a much higher plane than I."

The doctor stood, shook Dad's had, and turned to Mom. He took her hand in his, smiled, and said, "If this is the worst we have to worry about, consider yourselves blessed."

Mom and Dad turned their attention to Brooks, petting him and gathering their things to leave.

The good doctor disappeared.

As they were leaving the office, Mom sensed Dad's disappointment. Trying to console him, she said calmly, "Five years is a very long time, you know."

Dad turned and said, "He should have at least ten—and that's the plain, ugly truth!"

Chapter 23
It Is What It Is

It took a little bit, but when Dad thought about it, five years was a long time. After all, Brooks was a special dog and could beat the odds. He'd been doing it all his life.

Mom and Dad pledged that this was their little secret, and they were going ahead with their plans to compete in agility. This meant Brooks and Dad getting their act together on those contacts.

Before they could get serious, one little thing remained. They had another trip to Dr. Mev to get the neutering situation taken care of. Brooks was getting a little confused over all the attention he was getting lately. It was one thing to be allowed to lick the broiling pan before it went into the dishwasher, but Dad not kicking him out of the Barcalounger when he came in to watch the Phillies just plain befuddled him.

Mom thought it best to wait a week so Brooks could put his hip evaluation experience behind him.

Dad worked on new ways to get over the contact problems. A suggestion was made by one of his instructors to divert away from the problem obstacles and focus on something else like the weave poles. It made sense; maybe they were working too hard on one thing, and something else would help their confidence. The weave poles were the choice.

Brooks only had partial success in the fine art of weaving. They worked on the poles a little to the point that he could go in and out with the poles fully upright, but he was very inconsistent. Usually, most beginning handlers saved them until last in their training because they were considered the hardest obstacles to master. Big dogs had a particularly hard time with them since it was unnatural for them to bend their long bodies around the poles, in and out twelve times. In USDAA, the poles were spaced every eighteen inches, and that wasn't a lot of area for a big dog like Brooks to work.

Dad had made a set of weave poles that they could work with at home, but if Brooks brushed up against a pole, it would dislodge and have to be reset. This made it harder to focus, since half the time was spent resetting poles, but for the week and a half prior to Brooks going in for his operation, they spent all their time on that one obstacle.

The night before Brooks was to go to the vet, Dad took him out and worked on a little jumping and some tunnel exercises. Staying away from the dreaded contact equipment, they continued their weaving exercises. He had been going in and out fairly well, but he needed Dad to direct him so he would not to bail out of the routine before completing all twelve poles. In and out, back and forth they went over and over, stopping occasionally to reset a downed pole. For fifteen to twenty minutes, they resisted the temptation to do something else.

On the last run before the evening was done, Dad didn't know when they'd be able to work on the equipment again. The healing from the procedure could take a couple of days to a week, and the last pass through the poles had to be a good one. He set his boy up and shouted, "Weave!"

Upon entering the first pole, Dad stumbled and fell, leaving Brooks on his own. As Dad sat on his butt, the dog continued through the row of poles in a focused, methodical fashion. Dad was speechless. In seven days, Brooks managed to master the weave poles. Instead of quitting for the night, he ran through the obstacle again to convince himself that he hadn't seen a mirage. It was no mirage, and Brooks completed the exercise four more times before Mom came out in response to all of Dad's shouting.

Dad said, "Call ESPN. Get the Goodyear Blimp. You won't believe this."

Mom looked down and watched Brooks plow through the poles like a boat knifing its way through water. She watched in disbelief as he passed through again for good measure.

"Wow," she exclaimed. "How did you manage that?"

Giddy as a kid on Christmas, he yelled, "He all of a sudden just did it on his own!"

Since Dad had to work the next day, Mom took Brooks to Dr. Mev. Going in the office that morning, Brooks never felt better. Confident from his successes from the night before, he sat in the waiting room and flirted with the girls in his usual outgoing manner. With a wag of his tail, he signaled to the female sheltie sitting across from him. "Hi, sweetheart. You're looking real fine." When he was called to the examination room, he pranced by a lady Dalmatian and wiggled his butt. "Yo, sweet mama. Let's get together sometime."

As self-assured and upbeat as Brooks was when Mom took him to the vet, the total opposite was the feeling when Dad picked him up late that afternoon. Upon leaving, he thought, *What happened?*

Groggy and lethargic, it took every bit of energy to make his way out to the truck. "It seems like every time I go in that place, I come out worse off than when I went in," he said.

It was bad enough that he had lost his manhood in there, but to add insult to injury, he was fitted with an E-Collar, better known as an Elizabethan collar. Brooks knew it better as a pet lampshade or the cone of shame. Brooks was mortified. Getting home was the only thing he wanted as he staggered through the waiting room, bumping into chairs, people, and other dogs. "Don't look at me," he growled. "This isn't me."

Upon arriving at home, Dad lifted his boy out of the vehicle and steadied him up the steps and into the house.

Mom was ready to make him as comfortable as she could. Standing in the background, Vanah was feeling bad that she hadn't warned her brother about what he was up against. Not that she could do anything about it, but at least he might have known what was happening.

As she made her way into the room to greet Brooks, all those feelings turned into mass hysteria. *What the heck it that thing on his head? Why is he wearing a lampshade? He looks like a crazy flower from* Beetlejuice.

As Brooks slowly made his way to his bed, Dad took the collar off to allow him to rest more comfortably. Except for being taken out to try to do some business, he slept the whole time, only moving to get a little more relaxed.

The night was more restless for Dad than anyone else. He decided to let Brooks sleep downstairs. It seemed like every hour, he was down checking on his boy to make sure he was okay.

When morning finally came, Brooks seemed a little better. Even though he was far from normal, Brooks did manage to eat a little. By evening, his appetite had returned. Things started getting back to normal. It had been a traumatic two weeks for everyone, but the bond between Dad and Brooks was so strong and was the foundation of what made them so great together.

Chapter 24
The End of the Beginning

Brooks's recovery was fast, a credit to how healthy he was. I don't know if it was harder on Dad or Brooks, but with the success they had with the weave poles prior to the operation, both had to resist doing anything strenuous until Dr. Mev gave the green light. After about a week, it was full steam ahead, and they had the rest of the summer to prepare for their first trial in the fall.

It was a fairly normal summer in the Philadelphia area. There were several ninety-degree plus heat waves, but the temperatures averaged in the eighties with little rain. That made practicing agility almost a daily routine. Dad's popularity at Keystone soared after he demonstrated how good Brooks could do the weave poles and the speed in which they learned it. He was now the official equipment manager, and whatever spare time he had from working his dog in practice was devoted to building new equipment. In addition, orders were coming in from people who wanted him to make equipment for them.

With all his work around the equipment, Dad started to become fascinated by the art of building courses. Upon his arrival at class, which was now taking up his Tuesdays and his Thursdays, he studied the sequences and courses Alana was setting up, since she had lots of experience designing courses. She enjoyed having him help out, since the large majority of the club were women who really had no interest in anything but working their own dogs.

Dad took it upon himself to get to the field early enough to set up sequences before Alana would get there in the hopes of her finding them good enough to use in that night's practice. More time than not, she was satisfied, and soon he was allowed to run a session on Saturday mornings.

He would set up different course sequences for anyone who wanted to work their dogs.

Mom warned Dad not to let all this extracurricular activity get the better of him, because Brooks needed to be his top priority. By the end of the summer, it had become apparent that he was spending more time with courses and equipment than practicing with his boy. The early successes they had were history, and though they mastered the performance of all the obstacles, the teeter, walk, and A-frame remained a struggle.

It wasn't until the arrival of a new student who hit the club by storm that Dad realized he had to get back to the basics and make better progress or he was going to be left behind. Dennis ran a cocker spaniel named Bart. It wasn't that his dog was that fast or flashy; in fact, he was average at best, but what made them stand out was that they were fast learners. In the span of three months, they went from beginners to having competed in their first trial and earned a qualifying leg. Brooks and Dad had been working for six months and were nowhere close to earning anything in the ring. Putting things in perspective, Dad could keep playing around with equipment, building all the courses, and continuing to fall behind in working out his contact problems or take his training a little more seriously and become the great team they set out to be.

Dad heeded the challenge and would make the fall trial that Keystone would host their first attempt at a qualifying ribbon. Mastering the contact obstacles became the number-one priority, and with that they solicited every training technique known to mankind to overcome their problem.

October was time to show what they had. Though Dad had gone to many agility trials with Mom when she competed with Vanah, this was his first running Brooks. Everyone was excited since this was the first time all four were going to be away from home for more than a day. Though they were going to be running in a trial, the trip felt more like a camping trip or vacation than a dog agility competition.

Unlike the day trips they had taken in the past to participate in the various shows with Vanah and Brooks, this event was a two-day affair. Mom went ahead and made reservations at a hotel that wasn't far from the trial site in Towson, Maryland.

The hotel wasn't even ten minutes from the trial and was very friendly toward pet guests. With a room on the third floor, Brooks totally enjoyed the elevator ride. Their accommodations were spacious and had two large beds. Upon arrival, both dogs made a beeline to the far bed to stake their claim. That was okay with Dad since he was too beat to bring their crates up from the truck.

By the time everyone had eaten and gone out for the night, it had gotten to be nine o'clock. The alarm was set for six—and trying not to sound like the Waltons with their good-nights—the lights went out, and everyone crashed for the night. It was the end of the beginning; by nine the next night, Brooks's first agility trial would be history.

Chapter 25
Time to Shine

Morning came quickly, and like clockwork, Mom and Dad readied themselves, fed both dogs, and were set to go without a hitch. With the event scheduled to start at eight sharp, they both managed to shower, dress, take the dogs out to do their business before and after they had been fed, and grabbed some coffee and bagels with time to spare.

Arriving well before the activities would start, Mom got everything set at their tent.

Dad made his way over to the main tent to see if he was needed. Since this was a joint trial between the Maryland club and Keystone, each member was expected to work in some capacity at the trial. Dad was the equipment manager, and since half the equipment being used in the event was his responsibility, he had to check to see if everything was in good order.

Since Alana and her boyfriend had towed the equipment down the day before, there was nothing he really needed to do but be on hand if they needed him for repairs.

With some time on their hands, Dad took Vanah and Brooks on a little walk to loosen up while Mom checked in and got the schedules for the upcoming events. She had entered both of them in a full schedule of events. Both were running novice standard runs Saturday and Sunday. Brooks was entered in jumpers on Saturday and gamblers on Sunday. Vanah was skipping jumpers and running gamblers on Sunday.

The trial would open with novice standard, and the thirty-inch jump height would be the first to compete. Mom confirmed their entry with the registration table, got their armband numbers, and checked in with the ring steward to let them know they were there. She also found out what order they were running in.

"Good," Mom said. "Van is running fifteenth." She would have some time to observe how the handlers ahead of them were running and possibly pick up some handling tips. "Oh crap," Mom said after seeing where Brooks and Dad were placed. Number one—right out of the box! Nothing could be scarier than to be running in your first dog agility trial and be the first to compete. Not only the first in his class, but the first of the entire trial!

"Oh my God," Mom screeched. "This is unbelievable." The odds were one in forty-seven that this would happen. When she got back to the tent, Dad had already put the dogs in their pen and was about to go out to look for Mom.

After hearing the news of the starting order, it was Mom who you could have knocked over with a feather. She couldn't believe how calm Dad was. In fact, he seemed overjoyed with the fact he could get it over with and relax the rest of the morning and up until the jumpers run late that afternoon.

"I had you figured all wrong," she told him. "I'd be a mess if I were running first, but good for you." She didn't know that Dad should have received an Oscar for his performance that morning because deep inside, his stomach was twisted tighter than a stick of licorice. Before Dad had time to let the situation get the better of him, the call over the PA for all novice handlers to assemble in ring one for a judge's briefing was heard.

There were close to seventy people assembled in ring one to hear what Judge Johnny Howell had to say. Stern and to the point, he described how it was going to be in his ring. There was to be no cursing in the ring. He and only he would be allowed to swear, since he was god almighty when he was judging. "If your dog soils the ring, you will be asked to leave, and the stewards will hate you for having to clean up your dog's mess," he declared. "I have allotted ample time for you to complete this course, and if I think you are taking too much time to accomplish an obstacle, you will be asked to move on."

Dennis was standing next to Dad during the briefing. "This guy needs to lighten up a little."

The judge looked Dad in the eye and said, "I heard that."

"Don't look at me," Dad shot back. "I didn't say anything."

Judge Johnny continued giving Dad the stink eye for the rest of his spiel. After all was said and done, Judge Johnny allowed everyone to walk the course that was now ready for inspection.

Dennis approached Dad from behind and commented, "Do you believe that guy? Who does he think he is, anyway?"

Dad said, "Would you shut your trap? He might hear you. Thanks to you, he's got it in for me because of what you said earlier."

Slapping Dad on the shoulder, Dennis said, "Aw, don't sweat it. The guy loves you." He made his way around the course and was not heard from again.

Having walked the sequence several times, Mom came up and asked Dad if he had things set in his mind for how he was going to run the course. He compared his strategy with hers, since they were running in the same class. When both were satisfied, they hurried back to the tent to prepare for their upcoming runs.

Dad was numb. "Nothing to do but qualify," he said. Hundreds of things kept running through his mind, but one thing stood out over all the rest. If he let Brooks get out in front, he would be impossible to control. "Stay calm and stay focused. We're going to do this thing. It's time to shine."

Brooks was cool as a cucumber and put all the things that were going on around him right out of his mind. To him, it was nothing more than running in practice.

When they made their way to the start line, Dad put his boy in a sit. With his hand in front of his face, Dad firmly commanded, "Stay!"

Dad turned and started toward a spot on which he chose to stand to give the command to go. But in that only brief second or two, something snapped in the young dog's head telling him this was a race and speed was the only thing that counted. The obstacles were only there to slow him down. He wanted to get over them as quickly as possible. Brooks tore off the line and out ahead of Dad, leaving him stunned.

Fortunately, he easily cleared the first two jumps with ease. A left entrance into a ninety-degree tunnel to the right sent the speeding Terv smack into the face of the dreaded A-frame. As Brooks was navigating his way through the tunnel, Dad had time to get himself composed enough to be in position to intercept his boy before ascending the frame. It was textbook handling on Dad's part, but he was hard pressed to go much further and maintain control. Try as he might to get Brooks focused on a slow approach, it wasn't to be. He leaped from about four feet in front of the up contact and landed almost two-thirds up the face of the obstacle. He leaped off the top to the ground about two feet beyond the bottom, missing the down contact zone and sinking their chances of qualifying in their inaugural run.

It was all over. In eight short seconds, their bid for that green qualifying ribbon went right out the window. Sure, there was the whole rest of the course ahead of them, but it meant nothing now that Brooks disqualified himself by missing the A-frame contacts. A lot of handlers would have just packed it in or gone through the motions to finish without embarrassing themselves further, but Brooks wouldn't let that happen. Sensing Dad's frustration, he stayed on course like he was on autopilot and ran the rest of the course in a blistering twelve seconds under the qualifying time, faulting only once on the dog walks down contact.

It was a beautiful thing to see. The final two-thirds of the run were spectacular to watch, but what made it even more special was that he didn't let Dad quit. Instead, he picked up the pace and forced him to press for perfection so that the missed contacts were overshadowed by how they performed the rest of the course.

At the end of the run, Dad didn't know what to think. All he knew was that they hadn't qualified. No matter how many cheers and congratulations they got for finishing so strong, it didn't make up for the fact that a loss is still a loss—no matter how you spell it. As they were making their way back to the tent, everyone they passed acknowledged how well they ran. Though he appreciated the pats on the back, they didn't erase that image that burned in Dad's mind of seeing Brooks launch from the top of the A-frame.

When they were halfway back, Judge Johnny called time from the next run he was judging and sprinted over to Dad. Stopping them in their tracks, he placed both his hands on Dad's shoulders, looked him in the eye, and said, "I have seen a lot of dogs run in my day, and I just wanted to tell you that dog of yours has more heart than any I've seen in many a year."

Looking over at his boy and back to the judge, Dad replied, "You think so?"

"If you don't think so, you have no business running him. You guys can be great if you just work at it. All I can say is don't give up." He ran back to the ring, turned, pointed his finger at them, and shouted, "I have my eyes on you. Now go knock 'em dead."

Dad held his head high and trotted with pride back to the tent.

Alone for the moment, Dad knelt down in front of Brooks and stroked his head. "What am I going to do with you?" he asked. "I think you teach me more than I teach you."

The dog handed him his paw and gave a panting smile.

Dad heard a voice in his head say, "Let me make you as proud of me as I am of you." He showered Brooks with well-deserved kisses. It was their time to shine, and they did it their way.

Chapter 26
Contacts? We Don't Need No Stinking Contacts!

With Brooks in his pen with a rawhide bone to keep him happy, Dad made his way over to the ring to watch Mom and Van perform. It had gotten quite a bit warmer than when Dad had run, and that wasn't good. Vanah never did well in the heat, and for a late October day in Maryland, it was unusually hot. By the time their number was called, she was feeling the heat.

Dad stood behind the ring to get a good view so he wouldn't miss anything. When Mom got the signal to go, her girl didn't. She tried with all her might to motivate Vanah, but she simply didn't want to be out there. Finally, when Mom was just about ready to give up, Vanah showed some life and slowly made her way through the course. Unlike her brother, she was very precise about her contacts. The A-frame wasn't a problem, but her speed was. When she finally made it across the finish line, she had missed qualifying by a hefty ten seconds.

Back at camp, Mom and Dad mulled over the results of their performances and tried to encourage each other with their highlights. They joked about how Vanah and Brooks were different as night and day when it came to agility. Where Brooks was likened to a Shelby Cobra (Dad's description), Vanah was more a pink Mary Kay Cadillac. Speed was Brookie's game, and elegance was Van's. Both were amused by the thought that if they could combine the two, they'd be unbeatable. Since that was impossible, they would have to learn from each other in their quest for a title.

With Vanah finished for the day, Mom made her way over to the main tent to see if she was needed. Dad was running Brooks in jumpers later that afternoon and took his camping chair over to ring two where the advanced dogs were running. Settling down in an out-of-the-way spot, he started a habit that he performed religiously at every trial, and that was to observe.

Looking and learning was the key to everything he did. Sitting alone, he would watch how the better teams handled the courses they were running. Watching those advanced teams run that day had him dreaming of the day Brooks and he would be running with the elite. It was nice to dream, but they first had to get through novice and open before that would ever be possible. It sure was a thing of beauty to watch.

His visit to ring two gave him some insight into how he might approach his upcoming jumpers run. One thing he knew was that he had to put his earlier run behind him and be assured that a course made up purely of jumps and weave poles would be a recipe for success. With his head full of all kinds of ideas, Dad made his way back to Brooks and began formulating his strategy for the upcoming event.

When Dad got the call to the judge's briefing, there was a different judge running the event. Judge Judy wasn't the stern sourpuss adjudicator from TV fame; she was a very attractive young lady with a very cheery attitude. There were no reprimands in her briefing; instead, it was a happy, fun speech.

When he was allowed to walk the course, Dad discovered that it was a variation of the one the advanced teams ran. With a few subtle changes, a very difficult master's course was transformed into a doable novice run. Several twists and turns were the same as what he had observed the advanced dogs doing. It was a good test to put into practice what he had learned.

Since Brooks was unproven in competition, there were many questions about how he would run in jumpers. The only thing on Dad's mind as he made his way to ring two was the heat. It was a good fifteen degrees warmer than when they ran earlier. Over the summer, they had practiced in hotter temperatures, but this was going to be a real endurance test.

Prior to being called into the ring, Dad ran Brooks over the practice jump a couple of times to get loosened up and to try a cool crossover move he had seen one of the advanced handlers do. Upon tripping and

113

about impaling himself with the jump standard, Dad bagged that idea for a more conventional approach, to the disappointment of Dennis who got a real laugh out of watching Dad's flub. Frustrated, he returned to the on-deck area and waited to be called into the ring. Brooks was feeling the heat and reacting in a much slower manner while he waited.

Brooks was sitting beside Dad in the shade of the canopy that was over the on-deck area.

"Brooks, you're up!" the ring steward called.

With a clear view of the action, Mom observed what happened next from the sideline. "It was like a switch was turned on," she explained. "One moment, Brookie was just sitting there in the heat, and next thing you know, boom, they were off and running. And I mean running! It was like they picked up where they left off in the earlier run. One, two, three jumps in a row. The big dog seemed to clear each thirty-inch bar higher than the previous one."

Dad was in good form as well, staying out front and guiding his boy into the weave poles, their favorite obstacle. Plowing through those poles so hard, he snapped one right out of the base, hurling it into the air. One observer who just happened to be passing by couldn't help but get caught up with the show and hung on to watch the finish.

If there was any question about Brooks running in the heat, it was answered with a red second-place ribbon and a rousing round of applause from all who witnessed it.

Even Dennis gave Dad a compliment in his own sarcastic way. "For style points, I give the dog a solid ten. I give you a five."

Dad said, "They're not judging me. They're judging the dog!"

Back at the tent, a steady stream of club members came by to congratulate them on the run.

Brooks seemed to know he had done well. He held his head high when folks admired the big red rosette of a ribbon. If one had asked him his opinion of their success that afternoon, he'd sum it all up by altering a famous quote from *Blazing Saddles*. "Contacts? We don't need no stinking contacts!"

Chapter 27
The Curveball

The success from their Saturday afternoon jumpers run was short lived. Chalk it up to overconfidence or just plain inexperience, but if they could strike Sunday's standard performance out of the books, that would be just fine by them.

What started out as a very promising day blew up in their faces. Dad should have known after gamblers that it was to be a very tough afternoon. Gamblers was a game with no set course. You get points for completing as many obstacles as you can in a certain amount of time. When time is up, you have fifteen seconds to complete a preset sequence of obstacles for bonus points. Whoever finishes with the most points is the winner. Most handlers really don't concern themselves with winning this game. They use it as a practice run for the standard course, which was being held later that afternoon. Brooks was led over all the contact obstacles, and he never hit a single contact. Talk about wild! He was all over the place. Mom figured that he had no real direction or sequence to run, and that's how Dad lost control.

Hoping to take advantage of a very doable standard course, Brooks again ran amuck. Dad's mind must have been somewhere else. Once his boy got out in front of him, he was faulted three times for going off course. A plethora of downed bars and no contacts made for a very ugly run indeed. Dad was so upset that he handed Brooks to Mom and ran onto the course to help the ring crew reset everything! The judge applauded.

Mom fared far better even though they missed qualifying by a single downed bar. Their time was much improved from the day before. All in all, it was a bittersweet trial for both. The ride back to Blooming Glen

115

was quiet, mainly because Mom was exhausted and Dad was pissed by his earlier performance. Nonetheless, that evening after they had settled down from the trip, they were already planning for the future.

In years past, the Maryland trial pretty much ended the agility season for the members of Keystone. There weren't that many members who could afford the time and expense of going south when the trial season migrated for the winter. Not only that, if you didn't have your own equipment and a place to set it up, practice was impossible because the club packed everything away for the winter.

Despite the dismal showing, Mom and Dad had a blast. The agility experience had become a way of life for them, and they couldn't get enough of it. They had enough equipment to set up a course in the backyard, and Dad was still adding to the inventory every chance he got. They decided to keep on training as long as the weather cooperated. They spent the winter months working sequences and doing just enough to not forget the basics. Occasionally, several members from the club would ask to join them when the forecast was favorable. To Dad's delight, agility lived on through the winter.

There was little doubt that the Christmas theme that year revolved around agility. Brooks had given up on ever getting a Barcalounger he didn't have to share. No, he decided to be more conventional and ask for his usual beer and pretzel menu, but his main request was an international ban on the yellow contact zones. I think Dad had a similar request, but it didn't matter. Brooks was now zero-for-three in getting his number-one item on his wish list.

Christmas became a little more special that year for Mom though. Just after the Baltimore trial, they started their winter agility training. Brooks and Vanah enjoyed being treated to a game of catch after they worked out. Vanah's hands-down favorite toy was her tennis ball. She could go for hours playing with that thing, and like her brother, she could catch a ball as good as any outfielder on the Phillies.

One afternoon, Dad worked both dogs on the equipment for almost an hour. Mom was out shopping, and Dad had no problem including Vanah in his workout with Brooks. When they concluded, both dogs went to get their tennis balls. Brooks was the first to return, and Dad threw the ball way down in the back corner of the yard for him. Vanah wasn't into the long bombs; she liked Dad to throw the ball in front of her and catch it on the first bounce. When he did, for some reason, she didn't see it, and it rolled far out into the yard. Usually she would chase down the errant miss and bring it back, but for some reason, she needed some help tracking it down. This happened several times, and he chalked it up to the bright sunlight.

A week later, a similar situation occurred. A little suspicious now, Dad asked Mom if she had noticed any change in Vanah's seeing things.

"No," she replied. "But I haven't been doing anything that would make me notice."

Dad brought Van and Mom to the backyard and demonstrated her inability to see the ball when it was thrown her way. Three out of five times, Vanah failed to notice it. It was enough for Mom to warrant a visit to Dr. Mev.

Mom immediately made an appointment and got her in the next afternoon. Upon learning what Mom was bringing Vanah in for, the doctor put her through several tests to confirm his suspicions.

"I'm not usually quick to jump the conclusions," he explained. "However, in this case, I'd bet the house on my diagnosis. I believe she has the early stages of PRA."

Mom knew a little about the disease, but she inquired further. "I know that's a retinal condition, but what is it exactly?" she asked.

"PRA is short for progressive retinal atrophy, an inherited condition where the cells of the retina deteriorate and cause blindness. It's a degenerative disease. Unfortunately, I know of no cure."

Mom felt like she had been punched in the stomach with the news. "So what do we do?" she asked. "There has to be something."

Dr. Mev sat back, folded his arms, and said, "First, I want you to get a second opinion. Though I'm 99 percent sure of my findings, I want to be sure."

Calling Van over, he gave her one last look, hoping he might see something that would change his mind. Reaching into his coat pocket, he charmed Vanah with a treat. Out of the other pocket came a prescription pad. "I'm writing the name of a specialist," he noted. "He's an expert on this kind of thing and has the facilities to test her and be 100 percent sure. I only hope he proves me wrong."

As Mom gathered Vanah and her things to leave, she turned and said, "For once, I hope you're wrong too."

Mom heeded the doctor's advice and took her to the specialist that week. The doctor's conclusions matched Dr. Mev's; Vanah indeed had

PRA. The only good that came from the visit was that she was still in the very early stages of the disease, and there was still time left to enjoy a normal life. Eventually, her vision would be lost to the disease, and there was nothing that could be done about it.

With Christmas right around the corner, Dad thought it might be nice to make their main gifts to each other an "Agility Blitzkrieg." They would enter every agility trial available to them that next year; knowing how much a title would mean to Vanah and Mom, it was the perfect thing to do. Mom loved the idea, and soon after the holidays, she contacted all the clubs that held trials last to make sure they had their address so they could be notified about upcoming trials.

A decision that had to be made was how to deal with Vanah in the not-too-distant future. They guessed from what the doctors were telling them that she had at the most one year where her vision would hold up enough to do the things Mom had planned, such as getting her novice agility title. After all, she only needed one more qualifying round. Mom wanted to go further and title in the next level, but the unknown was how much her deteriorating eyesight would play in her endurance. Coupled with shutting down in the heat, things weren't looking good. For now, they were just going to look forward to a very busy 1995 trial season and make the best of it. As for the future, who knew?

Christmas had a special meaning for Mom that year. Even though Vanah knew nothing about PRA, she knew there was something very wrong with her. Experiencing all those tests and seeing as many doctors as she did had her scared, but knowing that Mom was by her side gave her all the security she needed to be strong and get through the things that were going on. All of that was instrumental in forging a special bond between the two of them that Mom held close in her heart.

Chapter 28
An Agility Blitzkrieg

Although the weather didn't cooperate as well as they wanted it to that year, Mom and Dad still got some practice with the agility equipment. Most of the time was spent on jumps and weaves. Occasionally the contact obstacles were brought out, but the workouts were really geared to keeping their interests up.

In January, Mom got a call from one of the club members at Keystone asking if she might be interested in joining them in an agility trial in Rocky Mount, North Carolina, in February.

"Damn tooting," Dad said. And so it was decided. They were going to their first out-of-region, indoor agility trial.

With less than two weeks remaining until the trial, Mom was able to secure an entry and get both dogs in for standard runs. The upcoming weekend would be the only time they had to get ready. When Dad got home that Friday night, he set up all the equipment in the dark by flashlight. He was out there for a couple of hours before he came in for dinner.

Where their heads had been the past couple of days was anybody's guess. Neither realized that the winter storm warnings had been issued for a reason. It was going to snow! By the time they awoke on Saturday morning, there were four inches in the ground—and seven more were coming.

On Saturday morning, people driving past the house on Route 113 scratched their heads and wondered why anyone would be shoveling their backyard in the middle of a blizzard. What they didn't know was Dad's determination to get some practice in even if it killed him. By noon, a disheveled and beaten man gave up and retired to the house. Mom consoled him with a hot cup of cocoa.

Relaxing in his Barcalounger, he flipped through the channels to try to find something on the TV to take his mind off the aches and pains from all that shoveling. By late that afternoon, the snow had all but stopped. Only a few flurries remained in the air, but the damage had been done. All the equipment was covered with close to a foot of snow, and the area that Dad had shoveled was covered by drifts. It was just like Dad to listen to the Weather Channel now that the storm had passed, but his motive was a logical one. He was hoping that the forecast would bring some warmer weather to melt enough snow to at least get the dogs out for one or two runs. No such luck. It would be too little to make any difference before they had to leave for North Carolina. Things just weren't looking up.

By morning, the plows had been out, and the roads were clear enough for Mom to go shopping. Dad had cleared off the cars and shoveled the driveway, and things were getting back to normal. She hadn't been gone more than ten minutes when he had gone up to the bedroom to change out of his wet clothes. While watching Brooks prance about the room and jump up on the bed like he was performing the pause table in agility, an idea sprung into his head. "Who needs a course outside when I can set one up here in the house?"

What greeted Mom when she got home from shopping would have won the ten-thousand-dollar prize on *America's Funniest Videos* if she had a video camera. The French doors leading into the living room served as the start line, followed by a jump set up in the middle of the room made up by a mop handle spanning from the lounge chair to the coffee table. A broom handle went from the other side of the table to the sofa, creating the second jump. Dad brought the small tunnel in and placed it—still dripping from melted snow—in a far corner. He found a piece of plywood and cut it to fit over the stairs with slats screwed every twelve inches, and he converted the steps to an A-frame.

Standing in the foyer utterly amazed, Mom heard thumping and barking coming from upstairs. Suddenly, in a blaze of activity, Brooks and Vanah roared down the makeshift A-frame.

Dad screamed, "Easy, Brooks! Touch the contact!" In an attempt to get down the stairs ahead of the two dogs, his feet went out from under him, sending him crashing to the landing in a crumpled heap.

Vanah and Brooks did not notice Mom standing in the doorway. They pounced on Dad and gave him kisses to express their joy and satisfaction over his stunt.

The trip to North Carolina didn't live up to what they'd hoped it to be. The long ride down with limited breaks was tough enough, and the weather didn't cooperate either. It was dreary, cold, and damp that weekend, and though it was far better than the blizzard conditions of Pennsylvania, it still left a lot to be desired. It rained most of the time, and practice outside was impossible. The only work they could get in was waiting in line to have a few sequences over a practice jump.

With the trial being held indoors, there wasn't enough room for x-pens. Brooks and Vanah had to be quartered in their crates at ringside or kept in the Blazer when they weren't running. They alternated between the two, and a favorable draw in the run order helped get them through a less than desirable trial.

Both dogs failed to score qualifying runs, but it wasn't a total loss. Vanah ran well enough to show Mom that her eyesight was still good enough to compete. She had a rare missed contact on the teeter and two downed bars, but the boost to morale was worth as much as a title to them.

Brooks was his usual wild self, still having trouble with the contacts, but the tight indoor conditions helped slow him down enough to have only missed three the entire weekend. Downed bars were also his problem that weekend, having knocked five of them off their stanchions, but the very sharp approaches due to the lack of space made it hard on all the large dogs.

The bright spot for Brooks was his continued unbelievable performance running the weave poles. It was getting to a point where spectators loved to watch him flash through the poles like they were nothing, but equipment managers hated it since they had to repair all the broken poles left in his wake. Nonetheless, Dad loved when people said, "Don't blink while you're watching him—or you'll miss him."

Brooks's fan club was starting to grow.

Even though the North Carolina trial netted zero qualifying rounds, a lot of experience was gained there. They also made a number of friendships. If they had it to do all over again, the only change would have been that they might go a day earlier to have some time to relax and prepare a little more.

With Punxsutawney Phil not seeing his shadow that year, an early spring arrived with great weather to practice in. Keeping true to their promises to blitzkrieg the agility schedule that year, Mom and Dad entered eight trials, which was considered a lot in those days. A number were out-of-town trials, but all netted the same result of not qualifying.

Danville scored five missed contacts and three downed bars for Brooks. Vanah missed one contact and downed three bars. Keystone's spring trial had Brooks missing four contacts and one downed bar, and Vanah dropped four bars and ran out of the ring in her final event.

Roanoke, Freyberg, Watertown, and Maryland all resulted in similar finishes.

It was getting a bit frustrating for both, and Dad didn't come close on any standard qualifying runs. Mom's compassion for Vanah's eye problems kept her hope running at a slightly higher pace. The PRA seemed to have leveled off; as long as she was happy in the ring, that was all the success she needed to keep on going.

Dad was sick and tired of hearing the same old phrases. "Think of all the experience you're getting. You almost had it that time." All he wanted to hear was the judge saying, "Score!"

Season two was in the books, and many of the same challenges that faced Mom and Dad from 1995 lingered into 1996.

Chapter 29
The Ever-Changing World

As busy as Mom and Dad were with participating in all those trials, 1995 was an even busier year at the club. Dog agility had become so popular that the club's membership had nearly doubled in 1994, and at the December board meeting, the issues of growing the club were addressed. Several new committees were formed, and they expanded the board of directors. Mom was asked to serve on the trial committee, and Dad was elected vice president. He also retained his equipment manager's position, mainly because no one else wanted it.

With all the structural changes—the expanded board, added committees, and increased memberships—Alana scored big in securing a new training location that gave them 24/7 access. It was speculated that Dad would be practicing with Brooks with a flashlight if he got the chance. Everything was good, and with the changes, 1995 saw the club grow as it never had before.

Dog agility was a hit, and southeastern Pennsylvania had become a hotbed of activity for the sport. USDAA still ruled as the more popular venue, but 1994 brought the AKC into the fold. They held their first sanctioned agility trial in Houston. This was great news to those agility-starved teams that were longing for more trials and matches to participate in.

It was long argued that USDAA was too demanding in its performance standards, primarily with its jump heights. The larger dogs were forced to jump thirty inches, and for a lot of dogs, it was a real strain to jump that high. AKC was now offering twenty-four-inch heights for the bigger dogs, and that piqued handlers' interest. They also lengthened the contact zone six inches, and I don't have to tell you what Dad and

Brooks thought about that. With those two changes alone, you'd think the AKC would gain universal acceptance, but it didn't.

Even though the USDAA had tougher standards, all dogs were allowed to participate in their events. The AKC was only open to purebred dogs. This caused a real problem at the club. Even though the majority of its members had purebred dogs, a third of them had mixed breeds.

Throughout that year, AKC agility became the hot topic. Even though no trials were held in the area, the subject came up as to whether Keystone should be the first club to host such an event. Those that had mixed breeds felt that they were discriminated against because their dogs weren't allowed to participate in AKC events. Why should they support a trial sanctioned by them? On the other side of the coin, handlers with dogs that struggled with the USDAA—and their tough performance requirements—felt they were discriminated against as well. The club was split mainly down breed, mixed-breed lines. However, both sides totally respected the other's argument. A civil war had broken out over the issue, and Dad got in the middle of it all.

It was no surprise where Mom stood on this issue. With Vanah's eyesight getting worse, they were running out of time in their efforts to title. With jumping being their main issue keeping them from qualifying, she welcomed AKC's entry into agility. Mom was so excited that she and several others in the club were in the forefront of having Keystone hold the first trial in the region.

With Dad, it wasn't that easy. Brooks was a performance dog, pure and simple. Though they welcomed the extended length of the contact zones, he didn't think it would matter that much. Brooks was allergic to yellow, and he wouldn't touch it even if it were made of peanut butter. So unless they got rid of contact zones altogether, the USDAA standards weren't an issue to them at all.

As for the AKC discriminating against mixed breeds at their events, he understood what they were all about when it came to responsible breeding and keeping things pure, but when it came to agility, he sided with the mixed-breed people. In Dad's mind, with over a hundred different breeds in the AKC's ranks, in order to get so many varieties, someone had to have mixed a breed or two somewhere down the line. Therefore, all dogs to him were mixed. Why not let them all do agility together?

Another consideration was his dog's well-being. Like Vanah, Brooks's time in the agility ring was limited. Knowing the condition of his hips, Dad couldn't help but wonder what the impact was from competing in so many trials and jumping at thirty inches. Though it wasn't a problem now, how much of a toll would it be on Brooks in possibly shortening his agility career or, more importantly, his life? Dad had practiced and competed with enough dogs to know how hard it was on a number of them to jump the thirty inches, and that alone had swayed him to support the AKC argument.

One other issue ate at him more than any other. It stemmed from a demonstration they had participated in at the Devon Horse Show in the spring of 1996. Equestrian people loved watching dogs do the canine equivalent of steeplechase. In years past, the founder of the USDAA, Ken Tatsch, would ship his organization's equipment to the event and ask Keystone to help work it.

It was chilly and damp when they ran the demo. The cold worked its way into their joints to make it downright painful to stand around. As far as Dad was concerned, it could have been zero out, and that wouldn't have bothered him in the least. He was going to be in the presence of greatness. Dad was going to run Brooks in an event held by the man, the guru. The infamous Ken Tatsch was the guiding light who brought dog agility as we know it to the USA. He was as much an idol to Dad in agility as Brooks's namesake was to him in baseball. This was to be the guy who would put them on the map.

Mom was totally amused by how Dad fell over himself helping with the equipment and volunteering to do anything and everything to impress his hero. To her, Mr. Tatsch was a good guy, and she was thankful to him for promoting the sport, but she drew the line at worshiping. Her objective was to have fun, but she was having a great deal of trouble doing so in the cold and rain. That didn't dampen Dad and Brooks's spirits. It wasn't every day that they got to play with a god. Ken must have felt a little strange when Dad asked him to autograph Brooks's head.

Brooks shined on that dreary day. Dad firmly believed that his usual pep talk prior to running had explained to Brooks who Ken was. Truth be told, Brooks really had no idea who that guy was. What had him all revved up was when they took to the ring, and he saw all those gold and blue Pedigree signs plastered all over the equipment. He thought he

125

was running in a bowl of dog food! That would be an item on his next Christmas list.

Unfortunately, the weather kept a lot of spectators away, but those who braved the rain saw quite a show. Ken had set up a fairly easy beginner's course and narrated each of the seven club member runs. Even with the rain, everyone performed well. They all would have earned a qualifying run if they had been officially scored. Only Brooks missed his usual down contacts on the A-frame. He did, however, make all the rest. To Dad, it was a successful run. What brought the house down was his weaves. After flying through the poles, Ken stopped them before they went on to the next obstacle. Addressing the crowd, he asked if they wanted to see that again!

After a resounding "yes," they wound up repeating it no less than five times, and the cheers grew louder with each run. Ever the showman, Brooks responded with a vigorous cheer of his own as he completed the remainder of the course.

"Wow," Ken said when they finished. "Do you mind if I give him a go?"

Dad didn't respond at first, thinking he was dreaming. When asked again, Dad responded with a resounding yes! This was the first time he had seen Brooks from a spectator's standpoint. As they ran the course, he never fully realized how fast he was. However, as great a handler as Ken was, even he wasn't good enough to get him to stop on those damned contact zones. That made Dad feel a bit better about how he ran.

Ken's reaction to Brooks was nothing but high praise. "You could have a world-class dog on your hands if you get him under control with his contact obstacles."

In the future, Mom had to keep reminding Dad of the word *could* when Ken referred to Brooks as "world class."

Everybody did three runs that day and delighted the crowd with all of them. Even though Brooks's weaves were the hit of the show, all the dogs, including Vanah, got a rousing response. Cold and tired spirits ran high later that afternoon as they struck the course and prepared to go home, but no one's emotional state was elevated to the altitude of Dad.

With everything packed up and ready to go, Mom went back to the truck with the dogs and waited for Dad. He stood out in the drizzle and talked to Ken. It's uncertain how long they were out there because Mom fell asleep and couldn't recall how long it was lasted. Somehow, Dad was invited to a judges seminar.

Ken was so impressed by Dad's involvement in the sport that he thought he had what it took to become a judge. It happened that a judges seminar was being held the following weekend in Massachusetts, and Ken wanted him to enroll. It would have been a no-brainer three months earlier, but Dad had been laid off from his job of twenty two-plus years in January, and the tuition was an expense they really couldn't afford. Upon learning of this, Ken offered to defray the cost if Dad could manage to get himself up there. It was an offer he couldn't refuse.

Dad managed to make good on the offer and made it to the seminar. The three-day affair brought out a total of twelve anxious handlers looking to be certified as USDAA judges. A heavy dose of rules and procedures took up the first day and was followed by equipment and course building on the second. He struggled a little with the rules, but he more than made up for it with his course-building skills. The third and final day was actual judging and evaluations, and that's where it all came crashing down.

Ever since the demo at Devon's, Dad had been suffering from a severe muscle pull in the back of his neck. It was likely brought on from straining himself in the cold and damp that day. It had gotten progressively worse as the week went on. The pain seemed to level off during the first two days of the seminar, but on the morning of the third day, it was almost impossible to get out of bed. Instead of receiving a certification to become an agility judge, Dad wound up going home with a prescription for muscle relaxers and orders to do nothing for a week.

When Dad got home that night, he was as depressed as anyone could be. What seemed like a sure thing had eluded him once again, and it was something totally out of his control. Though Mom tried to console him with the assurance that there would be another opportunity, it was little consolation. All he wanted to do was go to sleep and put it all behind him.

That night, he closed his eyes and tried to sleep, but he couldn't get the vision of himself being at the judge's evaluation out of his mind. As he tried to sleep it off, he felt the weight of something pounce on the bed beside him. Still in pain, he slowly turned his head to see what it was.

Brooks was beside him. Feeling his best friend's anguish, he tucked his long snout under Dad's chin and proceeded to give little licks to try to comfort his hero. Canines know when their people are hurting, which is an instinct that separates dogs from other pets. It was interesting how an ounce of kisses could wash away a ton of pain.

The next day, Ken Tatsch called to find out how Dad was doing. He reassured him that he always had an open invitation to attend any upcoming judge's seminar, and he would see to it personally that Dad would be given credit for his past accomplishments. It was something Dad never took advantage of. Maybe it was the lack of seminars venturing back to the area or his busy schedule that kept him from pursuing his dream. None of those reasons held water. He believed he would have had a hard time supporting the AKC movement Mom so passionately believed in if he became a USDAA judge. Even so, another opportunity for greatness was lost, and he chalked it up to the ever-changing world in which he lived.

Chapter 30
The Little Club That Could

It was a sub-zero night in February 1996 when the trial committee at Keystone held an emergency meeting to get a final vote to decide if they were going to hold an AKC trial or not. Running out of time to get the application in—and tired of all the debates over the issue—they managed to get plenty of members out to the new indoor facility they were leasing for the winter to train. Their hope was to get enough people out so they could get a quick meeting in for a vote prior to working the dogs.

It was a risky gamble that worked. They had enough members to have a quorum, and the measure passed with a unanimous vote. Mom had been pushing for this moment for close to a year. She was amazed that with all the dissension brought on by wanting to have the trial, so many braved the freezing temperatures.

A key figure in their success was a board member who had gotten off to a rocky start with Mom when she joined the club over some stupid thing neither could recall. Tracy knew the bylaws and "Robert's Rules of Order" better than anyone around. She and Dad were the ones who came up with the plan to get the members out that night and understood what the trial meant despite their personal feelings about the AKC. The trial was now going to be a reality, but the hard part was still to come.

When the club held the USDAA trials, it was a requirement that all members worked the trial. It was agreed that even though the full membership benefited from the revenues brought in by the event, the requirement was waived in respect to their political views on the AKC. Also those with the most experience wouldn't be participating. Nonetheless, they pressed on and made the best of what they had.

When the trial finally opened for entry, it filled up in three days. Handlers from as far south as Florida and north to New Hampshire entered. Upon hearing that the trial had sold out, the AKC decided to send two top officials to monitor the trial and make sure it was going to be run under their standards.

The pressure was really on now. Though the paperwork was twice what they were used to, it was getting done. The biggest task was what they called the grid. The grid was a matrix that organized the workers and let the ring stewards know who was working in the rings. The hard part about making it up was that the majority of those working the trial were running dogs as well. Conflicts were common, and it became an unbelievable nightmare to coordinate. Stepping up to the task was another new member named Connie. She got her baptism by fire, running trials, helping out with the grid, and volunteering her husband and two daughters to help.

Tracy, Connie, Brook, Robin, Mom, Dad, and six others were able to make themselves look like three times their number and created a success out of what most predicted would be a colossal disaster. And they did it under the scrutinizing eyes of the AKC.

The aftermath was bittersweet. Those who worked the trial were proud of their accomplishments, and the many who participated in it vowed to come back for the next one. But would there be another? If the anti-AKC folks at the club had any say, there wouldn't be. At the club's next general meeting, little was made of the trial. There was just a polite mention that it was held, and more important issues were addressed to pretend it never happened. The group that pulled off the impossible was given the cold shoulder for their efforts, and just like that, nobody cared.

After a couple of weeks, Dad received a phone call from a member who had gotten through the beginners at Keystone fairly well but was having some major troubles in the novice class she had advanced to. It seemed she was driving forty-five minutes to the club and getting little or no attention from the teachers with her German shepherd, Theo. Linda lived within ten minutes of Blooming Glen. Hearing that Mom and Dad had folks from the area come over when they weren't down at the club to train with them, she hoped they might be included. Practically in tears, she explained that several instructors from her class had said her dog didn't have what it took to run in competition, and they were wasting their time coming all this way to train. Hoping Dad might help them out, Linda became Dad's first student. She was also the inspiration to have it out once and for all with Keystone.

Dad and Mom had discussed the feasibility of splitting from the club. The way they were being treated after the trial—and several other stories like Linda's—told him their agendas were not in sync. Tracy planted the idea in Dad's head to start a new club from the group that ran the AKC event.

After a number of sleepless nights weighing the pros and cons of starting their own club, Dad decided to take Tracy up on her idea. At the next board meeting, Dad was like Jimmy Stewart in *Mr. Smith Goes to Washington*.

"You have taken the fun out of the sport," he proclaimed. "This club was built with the hearts of our dogs in mind so we can enjoy their willingness to please us in an activity we both enjoy. Turning dogs away because they don't have what it takes to compete is driving us from what this is all about." He handed the secretary his formal resignation and left the meeting.

Arriving at home after a forty-five-minute drive, Mom greeted him with a message from a former board member. After his dramatic exit, Tracy had a similar departure. The message simply asked, "What do we do now?"

Mom asked the same question, and Dad said, "Let's have a party."

That's just what they did! The party they planned was to announce the start of a new dog agility club and pledge its independence from Keystone. The event was appropriately held on July 4. It was a picnic, and nine of the members who ran the AKC trial earlier that spring attended with their dogs. Though they wouldn't conduct any official business, it was suggested by everyone that Dad be its first president and Tracy be the vice president. Other than that, the whole affair was devoted to having fun with the dogs.

They played long into the evening, only stopping to get a quick burger or hot dog. Everything from throwing tennis balls to challenging one another with wacky sequences with the agility obstacles was enjoyed. It all culminated in a final challenge for Brooks to run Dad over the obstacles. I think everyone agreed that the dog was the better performer.

Before everyone's departure, Dad gathered everyone and thanked them for coming out. "After all we've been through the past couple months and all that we have accomplished, I'm convinced we can do anything we put our minds to. If you don't have heart, you aren't living your dream."

Tracy said, "It's the little club that could."

Mom added, "The little club that did."

Chapter 31
Dogs in the NBA?

It took awhile for the new club to get fully organized, but that didn't keep people from working with their dogs and even entering a trial or two in the meantime. Mom and Dad still ran in the USDAA trials, mainly because it was the only game in town. They ran into the old gang from Keystone from time to time. Other than the few from the board and several hard-nosed anti-AKC folks, most of the general membership missed them. Dad thought they mostly missed Brooks and his weaves. Titles still eluded the two, and it was just a matter of time before they would only run AKC.

One day, Dad was listening to sports talk radio at work when he heard that the Philadelphia 76ers basketball team was having tryouts for a halftime program at their games. At first, he thought nothing of it, but a thought struck him on his way home that night. *Why not come up with a demo that they could try out for?* That would certainly put them on the map. He saw a dog at the Phillies game performing Frisbee routines, and it was a real hit. After discussing it with Mom and several handlers who were training with them, they all liked the idea. They needed more to go on.

The next day, Dad called the 76ers. Much to his surprise, he wound up talking with the president. The halftime gig was Pat Croce's brainchild; he wanted to showcase local talent during the fifteen-minute intermission between halves of the game. Pat was electric over the idea of having dogs perform, but two problems had to be solved. First, could Dad come up with some kind of routine for all the dogs that would be entertaining and could be set up, performed, and taken down in less than fifteen minutes? A second, more serious challenge was the timing.

It was Friday, and the final audition was on Sunday at two o'clock at the Spectrum, which was forty miles away. Dad figured if he could pull this feat off, then he could brag that the "Little Club That Could" had done it again.

On Saturday, he challenged Mom and Tracy to round up as many handlers as they could, even if they had to persuade some friendlies from Keystone. Dad spent the day roping off the backyard to resemble a basketball court and then came up with a routine that fans would enjoy.

After much thought and experimentation with Brooks over certain sequences they'd run in past gambler competitions, he finally struck the right chord. They would do a relay race on identical parallel courses. To make it easy to set up, a jump, a teeter-totter, a tunnel, and a set of weave poles would be used in each course. There would be eight helpers, each taking an obstacle to a designated spot, setting it up, and then standing off to the side, ready to reset the equipment if it were dislodged during the run. It was figured that they had up to five minutes to get everything set up. They could do the run for five minutes, leaving five minutes to get out of Dodge.

It was perfection to a tee. It could be set up and taken down quickly, and the race would be fast and furious. They would begin with the smaller dogs and work up to the big guys. At the start, they'd go over a jump, followed by the teeter. Next, the dogs would go through a 180-degree tunnel, sending them back toward the start line. The finale would be the weaves to the finish. The only question was if Mom and Tracy would be successful in recruiting enough people and dogs to pull it off.

Successful they were! Ten dogs and handlers were ready to invade their backyard at eight the next morning. On top of that, four were bringing their spouses to work as the ring crew.

Dad couldn't be happier. As pumped up as he was, he didn't sleep a wink that night. He was short a teeter and had to spend the time converting his dog walk into a seesaw.

Running on fumes that Sunday morning, he briefed everyone on the program and put it into action. Chris, one of the handlers who ran a spark plug of a terrier called Roscoe, had her husband bring his video camera and record the entire practice.

Tracy opted to MC and run her dog Torrey, and Mom found an old recording of "Wipe Out" to play on a boombox while they raced.

They ran and ran and ran until they had the right combinations of dogs racing against each other. The object wasn't so much to race but to have everyone end more or less together so the two anchor dogs could bring the house down as they weaved to the finish line.

It was no stretch that Brooks would be one of the anchor dogs since he set the standard for weaving. Little did anyone know that there was another dog just as good as Brookie. Her name was Bridget, Batteries Not Included. The only difference between the two—other than Bridget being a sheltie—was that she was six inches shorter. Both were speed demons on the course; if timed right, it would be the perfect ending to the show.

With their audition scheduled for two that afternoon, Dad had to halt the practice at noon to get everything loaded and arrive at the arena no later than one thirty. It was an uneventful trip, and everybody made it with plenty of time to spare. Security directed them into the building so they could unload their equipment, and they were allowed to park in the players' parking lot. Everything was set up, and all they had to do was wait for the remaining acts to finish.

Dad and the guys stood at the entrance portal and watched the final act conclude—and not a second too soon.

"That's the first time I ever witnessed the *Jane Fonda Workout* done to rap music," he proclaimed.

"We'll call you if we need you," the judges said after fifteen minutes of sweaty calisthenics to the tune of "yo, yo, mo, mo, fo, fo!"

Behind them, the judges looked as if they had gone through a workout of their own. They said, "Let's get the dog people out here, and call this thing over."

Dad's stomach started to churn. They were the last to audition, and it looked like the judges just about had enough of Mr. Croce's folly. As everyone was standing around and waiting for direction, an annoyed voice yelled, "We're waiting!"

Dad said, "It's showtime, guys. Let's do it like we did in my backyard."

Springing into action, the helpers set the course twice as fast as they ever had in practice. The handlers and their dogs lined up like they were an army drill team ready to hit the floor. Tracy introduced each member as they came onto the court to ready themselves for the big run.

It was a blur to anyone who ran that afternoon about how they got through the audition, but after practicing the routine so many times that morning, it was second nature. All they knew was when they heard that ominous laugh followed by the words "Wipe out" blaring out of the PA system, it was time to get it on!

First off the blocks were two Pomeranians. What Pippin and Feather lacked in speed, they more than made up for in entertainment value. They ran to the end of the teeter and rode it down to the ground like an elevator. Burt the beagle and Roscoe the terrier were next, and they put down nearly perfect runs. Callie the golden retriever and Flame the sheltie were an obvious mismatch in size, but they both finished in a virtual tie to bring on Keeper, a Bernese mountain dog and Brussel, another golden. The finish had the Keeper way out in front, having taken advantage of Brussel's stop-and-smell-the-roses approach to the tunnel.

It appeared that it was going to be a blowout for Team Bridget. She was just hitting the teeter when Brooks exploded off the line, caught her with his patented launch over the down contact of the teeter, and pulled ahead. The quicker sheltie took a slight lead at the exit from the tunnel, benefiting from the mighty Terv's manhandling of his tunnel run. Brooks slammed into the tunnel so hard that he knocked the spotter, who was there to keep the obstacle stable, flat on his back.

They couldn't have scripted the finish better. The two flashiest dogs battled it out through the weave poles toward the finish line. In the end, Team Bridget took the day after Dad tripped over his own two feet in the sprint to the win. Brooks never crossed the finish line, as he reared back at the last second to aid his fallen leader. The building erupted as the few hundred people who were spread throughout the arena filled the seats behind the judge's bench to witness this strange race. It made the ten that ran feel like they had won a championship.

As Dad sat on the floor of the Spectrum and listened to the cheers, time stopped for a moment. Even though it was only an audition, he knew the few who watched the "Little Club That Could" that September afternoon would soon forget what they had accomplished in such a short amount of time. However, only he and his dog would know what really happened that day.

As driven to compete as Brooks was, the only way he wanted to cross that finish line was with his hero. Together they won, and together they didn't—and that was something they never forgot.

Chapter 32
Another Place at the Table

Soon after the audition, Dad received a call from the Sixers organization. They had been selected to do a halftime show during a game in November against the Phoenix Suns. Unfortunately, before they could even get one practice in, the program was canceled. It seemed the rap group had been selected for one of the exhibition games and were so bad that the crowd rioted. Fearing that other acts might fall victim to the same fate, they wound up canning the program.

Dad was very disappointed about the news, but there was always something to keep him pressing on. The new club called themselves "The Kruisin' Kanines." There was no mystery on how they got that name or who designed the logo of a dog driving a convertible over a teeter-totter. There were twenty members and just about every one of the original ten members was on the board of directors or served on a committee.

Even with a lot of time spent on growing the club, Dad managed to find time to bring one of his favorite hobbies back into his life. While some people claim they can communicate with their dogs through physic means, Dad did it by making Brooks as human as he was—at least on paper. Dad really had a knack for living in his dog's world and making it human. That's why they communicated so well—with the exception of touching contact zones. It was also his form of release from the aggravations of entering so many trials and never getting a qualifying ribbon in standard competition.

Dad wrote a Brooks World article for the club's first newsletter and surprised everyone with its announcement.

137

Well, Mom and Dad have really done it now. They got me another sister right when I figured out my other sister Vanah, and all was right with the world. Now I have to start all over again.

They call her Samantha. I call her spoiled. She has her own crate with more toys than Toys"R"Us. Mom got her this fancy collar that looks like something a human would wear. It's plaid!

Nevertheless, I have to say she's a looker. Those long skinny legs and sexy butt are a real turn on. I think in time we can be friends, but I have some real work to do. She has some really bad habits. She's into this women's lib thing, and it annoys the hell out of me. When Dad and I are watching the Eagles game, she won't get me a beer when I ask. When Dad and the guys are talking Flyers or Sixers, she yawns and howls just to be rude. I don't burp when Mom, Vanah, and she talk about the goings on with All My Children. *I wait until they're done. She even steals Dad's tools and hides what she can't chew up.*

What really frosts my oinker roll is that she thinks she can do agility better than I can. Those are my toys out there, and if she thinks she can compete with me, well, we'll see about that. Let's get real. Just because Samantha learned the dog walk in one hour or did the A-frame on her own the first time she saw it, it doesn't make her a master agility dog. It's taken me years to get to the level I'm at. Heck! I bet she can't jump over contact points better than I can.

In reality, Brooks delighted in having a new sister. Like Vanah and Brooks, she was a Belgian Shepard, the same breed as they were but a different variety. She was known as a Groenendael; the main difference was her shiny black coat. Everything else was much the same as the Terv.

She came to Mom and Dad shortly after Vanah finally titled. Even with the busy schedule they were keeping by working with the new club, a few AKC trials had opened up, and she went three-for-three in qualifying. It's amazing what the difference in the jump height made for her.

138

Van's final trial turned out to be a quite a cliffhanger. Having trouble seeing the bar on the last jump, she hopped over it and brushed the bar. Thankfully, it stayed up just long enough for her to cross the finish line and stop the clock with a qualifying score and a title.

That would be Vanah's last competition, since her eyes progressively worsened afterward to the point that it was hard to make her way around the course without crashing into things. For once, things worked out as planned. She would have liked an advanced title, but they were happy nonetheless.

With Vanah officially retired, fate took a strange turn for the better. A member of the club had a friend who was looking for a home for a Belgian Shepard. Peggy and her husband had several themselves and would have loved to bring this girl into their fold, but they just couldn't. Hearing that Mom might be looking forward to getting another dog, they approached her, and the rest is history.

Her name was Sarafena, and not a sweeter dog existed, with the exception of Vanah and Brooks. It was love at first sight, and with that, she became part of the family. Sara came from an abusive family, and upon hearing the atrocities she had gone through, it was everything to keep Dad from committing a capital offense on her former owners. In fact, Dad had put out a very strong warning that if he ever got wind of anyone giving them another dog, he'd personally take it away. Dad was a peaceful guy, but when it came to animal abuse, he became really ugly.

In an attempt to put things behind her, Sarafena became Samantha or Sammy for short. Vanah understood about getting a new sister, much to Mom's surprise. Usually two females have trouble getting along, but it was almost like she knew Sammy had it bad and welcomed her with open paws.

Brooks had a little trouble adjusting to the whole thing. In everyday situations, he was a real gentleman and even allowed her to try out his Barcalounger. However, when it came to agility, he was used to getting all the attention—and that's where he drew the line.

Dad had Brooks pegged in his newsletter article about Sammy learning the contact obstacles almost overnight, and that didn't sit well with him. Brooks would bark and carry on when Sam was on the course; he even went as far as to follow her up the dog walk in an attempt to distract her. Dad had to chase him down to get him put in the house so Sam could work in peace.

Nothing Brooks was doing was helping, and he was getting desperate. When the 1997 season opened up, it was time to be bold. For the first trial of the season, Dad entered his boy in an event in Freehold, New Jersey, eighty miles away. Mom wasn't feeling well, and she and the girls passed on the trip. The whole ride took close to two hours, and Dad prayed, pleaded, yelled, and sang to Brooks to get him to understand that he had to slow down for those infernal contacts. He even sang "Goodbye, Yellow Brick Road."

The event meant a little more to Dad than most because his old nemesis was going to be there. It would be the first time he would compete against Dennis since leaving Keystone. Dennis didn't get embroiled in all the politics that had split the club. He chose to let everyone else fight the battle and sided with the winner. Meanwhile, he had racked up some impressive titles, which added to the lack of humility he carried so proudly.

"Still running novice, I see. Good luck with that," Dennis quipped.

Dad could only smile and say thanks.

"No pressure, Brooks," Dad said as they made their way to the start line. "Just give me one good run. That's all I ask." Dad felt Dennis's eyes burn into his back as he put his boy in a sit and started to make his way out to the first obstacle. He whispered, "Is Sammy a better agility dog than you are?"

The result was an astonishing second-place finish—and the elusive green qualifying ribbon graced his day.

Dennis went home with a rare DNQ on his scorecard. It seems that he was too busy paying attention to Dad and had forgotten to walk his dog. Soiling the ring was grounds for not qualifying.

The ride home that evening was reminiscent of those days in obedience when qualifying was a common occurrence. It had been ages since Brooks had gotten his traditional Happy Meal for being victorious, and it was good. What really made it all worthwhile was that he was the king of agility in his house that night.

Chapter 33
Weaving into History

It didn't take long for Brooks to get back to his old ways with the contacts. Now that more clubs were forming and holding AKC trials, 1997 was a banner year for trials. It wasn't until midsummer that Sammy was ready for her first trial, but in the meantime, holding demos was one of Mom and Dad's favorite things to do.

Demos allowed everyone who would participate an opportunity to relax with their dogs and run agility without the pressure of having to qualify. It also allowed them a chance to show off their talents and expose the sport to those who had never seen it. In short, it was a great big ego trip for handler and dog.

Dad loved that it got the creative side of him going. Nothing charged his batteries more than outdoing a past event. The Sixers audition was a demo of sorts. Dad always made that event the benchmark for all others. Its simplicity and ease to set up and run made it perfect to show off and have fun. The club started getting more and more to do because when the Kruisin' Kanines ran a demo, they rocked!

One such demo was at Tracy's place of employment, a retirement home. The activities committee was always trying to find things for the folks who lived there to do. *Why not treat them to a dose of agility, Kruisin' style?* The basics of the event were similar to the Sixers, but they had a little more help and more obstacles were added.

Tracy came up with a narration that would allow the crowd to participate by having them choose who would run against one another. Since the average ages of the residents were prehistoric at best, Dad elected to change the music from "Wipe Out" to "Swing, Swing, Swing" from the 1940s. He added an equally fast-paced instrumental and a classic drum solo. It was perfect for the crowd and for the handlers since the song was three times as long, and there were four times the dogs running than at the Spectrum.

The show was a hit. They ran far longer than planned because each team would tie the other, and neither could break it. With Bridget and Brooks dueling the weaves, it was hard to imagine so much cheering coming from people so old.

One orderly commented that this event put more smiles on their faces than Bob Hope could. The Kruisers admitted that it was as heartwarming an event as they had ever done. Always the showman, Brooks had to steal the show by flubbing his final run. He broke for the fire escape, chasing a nurse into the building and down to the cafeteria. He got a stale breadstick for his effort.

Though demos were fun, and they had their purpose, the business of titling went on. That year, Brooks and Sammy traveled all over the Mid-Atlantic. Aside from the four events in the Philly area, they attended trials in Charlotte, North Carolina; Winchester, Virginia; Westminster, Maryland; Freehold, New Jersey; and a special event in Syracuse, New York.

Syracuse was a USDAA trial they had to be talked into doing. With Dad still building agility equipment, the club holding the trial had contracted him to furnish several PVC jumps he had designed. Having more orders than he could get out, trialing took a backseat for a couple of weeks so he could get caught up.

One of the judges for the event was a woman from New Hampshire who owned one of Brooks's cousins. She had heard about a Terv in Philly who was simply marvelous with the weaves. Her dog was equally as talented, or so she thought, and she designed a weave pole challenge to see who had the fastest dog on the poles. It was to be held in the evening after the first day of competition, and all were invited to compete.

After long nights of trying to get his work done, his remaining customer told him his order could wait and that the challenge was more important. It was decided. They would indeed attend. The only rub was that the customer waiting for his jumps demanded two more if Brooks didn't come back a winner.

The trial at Syracuse was the typical bust, no qualifying run, though he did get a second in gamblers. At the end of the day, the courses were struck and everyone broke for dinner. The Great Weave Pole Challenge would commence at eight. Forty-eight poles were lined up just outside ring one. What a sight it was. The rules were simple: the dog who completed the challenge the fastest would be crowned champion, plain and simple. If a dog missed a pole, they could correct the mistake, but they had to do them all to have the time count.

Twenty dogs of all shape and sizes were there. The dominant breed was the border collie with five, followed by the golden retrievers with three, and the Tervs with two. Some competing were there as a joke, like the basset hound and an older-than-dirt Clumber spaniel who seemed to trip over his own ears because they were so long. One surprise dog that was entered and was dead serious about challenging the borders was a microscopic Chihuahua. His name was Bolder, and like his name, the handler ran like she was stoned, but the little guy had the time to beat going into the eleventh competitor.

Most of them put up very respectable times with hardly any corrections. Dad was concerned because he had no idea they were doing so many poles. The most Brooks had ever done was the standard twelve; without the opportunity to practice, it was a pure crapshoot as to how they would do. They had six stick-in-the-ground poles they could warm up on, but other than that, it was going to be really interesting how it was going to turn out.

Brooks was running seventeenth with the other Terv, a golden, and a border rounding out the field. It was predicted that they were the ones to beat, but Dad was very nervous as he stepped up to the line to do the pass.

"Go when ready."

Dad and Brooks were off. Dad kept pace just ahead of his boy. He could feel the exhilaration build as the dog wound his way back and forth through each pole. With each thrust of his hips, his shoulders countered, driving him down the line. The timer quivered when she peeked at the stopwatch to see the fastest time she had ever witnessed. At pole forty-two, he missed. The crowd knew they were witnessing greatness and held their breath as Dad guided him back without going too far ahead of the missed pole, correcting the run and losing less than a second.

The excited timekeeper yelled, "10.124 seconds! That's the new leader in the clubhouse by 2.35 seconds."

The crowd was speechless. The dog who had formerly been in first place was a local favorite and had done this before. Brooks had knocked

143

him out of the race by a blistering two seconds. With three to go, it would be a nail biter for sure.

Brooks's new rival Terv was up next. Dad crossed his fingers as he watched the younger female mimic his run pole for pole. The first difference was that her run was without fault. The other difference was that she was now in second place, a full second and a half behind Brooks.

One down, two to go. The golden who was thought to be a contender proved to be a pretender by blowing past three poles and bailing out at pole thirty.

"One more and the title's yours," Mom whispered. Grabbing Dad's arm, she must have squeezed all the circulation out of it watching the last dog perform.

Stumbling into the first pole, the final dog gained his composure and posted a 10.010 time. In any other competition, that would be classified as a tie, but .114 seconds was an eternity in agility, and that was the border's margin of victory.

In the spirit of good sportsmanship, the owner of the border insisted the challenge be declared a tie, and both dogs were declared 1997 weave pole champions. She admitted that if Brooks hadn't missed the forty-second pole, he'd have been the sole champ. That event became the cornerstone of everything Dad preached from that day on about sportsmanship in agility. It wasn't about winning the title that the handler was there for; it was having fun and appreciating a good competitor.

Later that year, Dad learned that the border collie they raced against had been stricken with hip dysplasia and retired. It was the first time he'd ever heard of the Rainbow Bridge; unfortunately, it wouldn't be the last.

Chapter 34
Our Boy in Florida

As busy as 1997 was, 1998 was even more hectic. Monday through Thursday had cars and minivans packed in Mom and Dad's driveway for lessons and practice. The first Wednesday of the month had the club meeting in the living room for a general membership meeting, and the board met on any given night at the end of the month. That year, the club's membership grew to over forty; business was booming for the Kruisin' Kanines.

With the club meeting and training at the house, it was starting to take its toll, especially with a full season of trials and demos. Other than traveling to out-of-town agility events, Mom and Dad hadn't been on a real vacation since they had adopted Brooks in 1993. It was time to shut things down for a week and get away from it all.

There's no better way of describing the adventure than the Brooks World that followed their trip.

Well, I'm back from vacation, and what a trip I had. Dad decided to go whole hog this time and leave the state of Pennsylvania. In fact, we went all the way to sunny Florida. Wow! Just think of it: the sun and the surf, high-rise condos, nightclubs, high rolling, and best of all, women in thongs. Hot damn! Not exactly.

I should have known better. The first hint that things weren't quite what I expected wasn't the fact that we drove. Riding twelve hundred miles in a Ram Diesel was so cool and nonstop too. The only thing that could be better would have been riding in a Kenworth. The problem was the girls.

"When are we going to get there?"

"I'm hungry."

145

"Where are we?"

Blah, blah, blah!

We stopped at every rest stop on I-95 just to use the facilities. If it wasn't Mom, it was my sister who had to go. At least when Dad had to stop, it was at a Waffle House. Eat and go, I say.

The next hint was how Dad kept his cool with Mom. So what if he got a little lost by winding up on the Atlantic coast when we were going to the Gulf coast. It was an honest mistake. They are both large bodies of water. At least, he knows when you're going to Florida from Pennsylvania that you don't go through Boston. What a guy!

When Mom kept telling him to stop and ask someone for directions while we appeared (and I emphasize appeared) to be lost, he did, and Mom never said anything again. The guy we asked had green teeth and hair growing on top of his nose! The only directions he knew were to Sow's Beer Emporium. Even I didn't want to go there. Beer or no beer, we pressed on.

The place we were staying was at a resort that one of Dad's electrician buddies owned. He said it was in Naples. Naples, Nacomus, what the hey! They both sound alike. It really wasn't that bad if you like old-fashioned living. They call it Seaside World. Mom called it Seizure World. It seemed the youngest person living there was a veteran of World War I, and Seaside World was a reenactment of no man's land.

Everybody was really quite nice. They all ride in these little golf carts and wave at you. Sammy and I got a kick out of chasing them until I got a ticket for speeding. The speed limit was only ten miles per hour. This one old gal got upset and chased Dad down because he didn't wave back. Dad thought he had given her the slip when he pulled the truck up behind what he thought was a Laundromat. Little did he know it was the bingo hall and the woman who was after him was chairlady of the Seaside Socialite Society. She made him play bingo and listen to Perry Como music for three hours. If that wasn't bad enough, when Mom found out, she threatened to rat on him to that old lady whenever he argued with her.

All in all, things weren't that bad. The weather was fantastic and oh, did I love the beach. And what a beach it was. Dad went out one morning to take me for a walk, and we happened to find a great beach that nobody was on. What a wonderful place to play Frisbee, we thought. We rushed back to the resort and got Mom and Sammy. Dad changed into his bathing suit, if you want to call it that. Rainbow-colored Bermuda shorts went out in the sixties with bell-bottoms. Mom wore a stylish one-piece suit while Sammy donned her bikini. I, the studly man-dog that I am, sported the Speedo look, and off to the beach we went.

Mom couldn't quite figure it out, but something was strange. After spending the week looking for a place that allowed dogs, let alone not being crowded, how did this place show up? Nevertheless, we proceeded to set up camp. Mom and Sam were content to work on their tans while Dad and I challenged the mighty surf with a game of Frisbee. As we worked our way down the beach, Dad launched a throw that the wind picked up and sailed way off in the distance and over a sand dune. Like an avid sports nut, I pursued it. What Dad couldn't understand was why I didn't bring it back. After a short time, he discovered why. From a distance, he noticed I had attracted a crowd. Thinking they were admiring me, the cute puppy that I am, he found it was I admiring them, and loving it. Little did he know that Mom's suspicions could never be realized. The highlight of our grand vacation was the discovery of Buff on the Bluff, a nudist colony!

Later, Dad explained why they didn't go on more vacations together. They'd never survive.

Chapter 35
Say It Ain't So

Brooks had been competing in agility for more than six years when they entered the 1999 season. He competed in countless trials with little to show in the line of titles. Other than in dog agility, he had a very impressive resume. He was a breed champion, had an obedience title, and was a canine good citizen and therapy dog. Unofficial titles included weave pole champion in eight unsanctioned club events, nine first-place showings at USDAA matches, four UKC first-place match titles, and innumerable ovations at demos.

Time was running out as Dad struggled with the constant reminder of the diagnosis the now-retired Dr. Mev had given Brooks five years earlier. *I believe Brooks has five good years in him to do all the things a normal Tervuren can and wants to do.* Those words haunted him every time they took to the ring.

At the beginning of the year, Brooks was given a clean bill of health by a new vet who had been recommended by his former doctor and told to keep his appetite in check. Any extra weight could be a strain on his hips and accelerate his condition. Brooks's stomach was never full, and satisfying his constant urge to chow down was next to impossible. He was the one who wrote the book on pillaging. Mom and Dad kept a close eye on him and continued to press on with a full slate of activities for the coming year.

One change Dad had made the year before that seemed to be a good one was to allow others to run Brooks at practice and certain trials. Though they had about the same result as Dad did, it gave him the opportunity to watch his boy in action. It also gave those who dared run him a taste of what he had been going through all these years.

Two of Brooks's favorite people in the club were Maureen and Jen. Aside from Mom and Dad, they were his best friends. Maureen, who would one day become a judge and run her own agility training center, had worked her way up in the club from a beginner student with her wild dog, Corkey.

Dad taught her all his mistakes and said, "Do as I say, not as I do."

At a trial in New Jersey, Dad handed Brooks over to Maureen out of frustration. They were having "one of those days." Dad seemed to be having more and more of them.

"Perfect on everything but the yellow," the judge said.

Thinking she could get Dad's boy through the problem, the next day he was hers to run. The result was that Maureen learned what "one of those days" was like.

Back at home, Brooks was getting impatient with Dad. He was spending more and more time working with other people's dogs and less time with him. One evening when no one was home to watch him except for Dad—and he was out back conducting a class—Brooks carried on so much that it disrupted Dad's instruction. Jen, the teenaged daughter of one of the participants in the class, volunteered to get the angry Terv so Dad could carry on with his lesson.

The two got along so well that when Jen wasn't helping her mother with her dog, Brooks became hers. A special bond between the two began to form, and before anyone knew it, she was learning agility with the wildest dog in the East. Though everyone loved to see Brooks do the weaves, Jen got a thrill out of watching him jump. The best photograph of him jumping was with her handling him.

Brooks ran in two events that year prior to Kruisin's spring trial. In both, he missed qualifying by only one missed contact in each run. Dad was very optimistic about their chances on their home turf. With the help of Maureen and Jen—who were determined to help Dad get a title—it seemed like a perfect scenario where the elusive title could be achieved in front of the home crowd.

Two standard courses—a jumper's and a gambler's run—were slated. Along with a full work schedule as the chief course builder, it would be a very hectic weekend. Knowing how important it was for Dad to do well, Jen's mom allowed her daughter to help him with Brooks. She would make sure Brooks would be ready when Dad took a break from his chores of working a trial.

Dad was always the first to arrive. On the day of the trial, he got there around five. He sat in the dark, sipping his second cup of coffee and contemplating how in the world he was going to get through a full slate of runs with his dog and build courses at the same time. This wasn't unusual for him; he had done it so many times that it was a ritual. This event felt different, but he couldn't put his finger on why. There wasn't anything out of the ordinary going on; there was just the hope that he would have a good showing in front of the home crowd.

Mom showed up with the dogs around six, and she too had a busy day ahead of her. Although her duties were more administrative than anything, they could be more taxing than the physical jobs. Taking advantage of a lull while they were waiting for the judges to arrive, Dad took Brooks for a walk in a secluded area within the park. After allowing him to run around a little to loosen up, he called his boy over and sat on a huge rock.

Brooks sat in front of him and listened as Dad gave his usual pep talk. "You've been doing really well lately, and I hope it carries through today. Even though a lot of familiar faces are going to be watching us, I know you'll do your best to make me proud, qualifying or not."

Brooks looked up at Dad and placed his chin on his knees, something he had never done before. He seemed to sense that this trial, for some reason, meant a lot to his hero. This time, he was going to do something special. Dad stroked his boy's head and looked into his eyes. He saw a sparkle that gave him hope that today would indeed be an extraordinary one.

The PA broke Dad's focus. "Jim, report to ring one. Jim to ring one."

"Okay, boy. Gotta go to work," he mumbled. They made their way to the tent, where Jen was waiting to take Brooks back to his pen.

For some reason, Brooks was running jumpers first but not until midmorning. Usually the standard runs were the first go, but Dad wouldn't complain. It would be a good warm-up for the run that really counted later that afternoon.

Ring one kept Dad busy throughout the morning, though he could break away for the judge's briefing for his jumpers run. Since there were schedule conflicts when they ran and Dad needed to be elsewhere, Brooks drew the last spot in the order. This gave him just enough time to get Brooks over to ring three, which was the farthest from where they were camped and ready to go.

When the time came, Jen had Brooks walked, warmed up, and ready to go at the starter's tent—and not a second too soon. Dad had gotten held up with some equipment issues and just made it in time to go on. He emptied his pockets of any goodies and strapped on his armband.

Jen handed Brooks over to Dad and gave him a rubber band to put around his wrist. "It's for luck," she whispered. Petting Brooks on the head, she said, "Give me five." He did, and Jen said, "I love you, Brookie." She was off to her vantage point in the hopes that he'd do well.

As they stepped up to the start line, it was like the world stopped. The few seconds it took for Dad to put his dog in a sit, stay, and walk out to the course to get position seemed like hours. It's amazing how little things from the past come into your head when you put yourself under pressure. For a brief second, Dad felt like he was back at the Spectrum performing for Pat Croce. As that thought passed, he said, "Brookie, jump!" And they were off.

It took less than a second and a half for Brooks to go from a sitting start to leaping over the first jump. Right from the moment the starter pressed the button on the stopwatch, everyone who was watching knew it was going to be a great run.

"It was as if he was on autopilot," Dad later described. "He knew the course, and my presence wasn't required."

I won't sell Dad short. His presence gave his boy the heart to outdo any run he had ever done. He performed jump after jump like they weren't even there. At one point on the course, he approached a trick right turn.

Mom was watching from the scorer's tent, and she observed him adjusting his body in flight so he could be in position to get over the next obstacle.

At no point in that run was there any question that Brooks was on his game that day, and the show he put on going through the tunnels made him look like he had been shot out of them. Though there are photographs of Brooks running that event, it's sad that no one had a camcorder, especially of the final three jumps. The straight-line sprint of graduated hurdles started with a single and ended with a triple. Though the finish line was ten feet beyond the last jump, Brooks cleared it with ease. He landed a foot over the line to finish fifteen seconds faster than the qualifying time.

Five seconds later, Dad finally made it across the finish.

Brooks was ready to maul him with kisses and hugs. He knew he had done well, and a number of club members gathered around to congratulate them on the fastest jumpers run they'd ever seen. What mattered most to Dad was that Mom, Maureen, Jen, and most of the Kruisin' Kanines were there to share in their triumph. It was a wonderful thing.

Unfortunately, the celebrations had to wait. There was much work to be done, and after Dad gave his boy a hearty congratulatory rubdown, it was time to make his way back to ring one.

Jen took the proud Terv for a little walk and then headed back to the pen.

At a little before noon, Dad noticed Jen at the opposite side of the ring. He was spotting jumps for the advanced standard class, and she was frantically waving to get his attention.

At the first break he got someone to take his place, he went to see what she wanted.

"You need to check Brooks out," she said, almost in tears.

"What's wrong? Is he okay?" Dad asked.

"I don't know," she said. "I just had him out for a little walk, and he started limping with his right rear leg."

Right rear leg. The words stung him like a million hornets. He suddenly recalled Dr. Mev's exact words. *His right hip is where you'll notice him having the most problems. That hip seems to be the worst.*

"No," Dad said. "He just stepped on a stone or something."

When he arrived, Brooks seemed totally fine and very happy to see him.

Dad tried not to show concern and wrestled with him for a bit. When they went over to an open area, he handed Brooks over to Jen and told her to walk him like she had done when the limping occurred. Back and forth they went with no noticeable limp. In fact, Brooks actually looked stronger than when they had run the jumpers event.

"I swear he was favoring his right rear," Jen exclaimed. "I know what I saw."

Dad said, "I believe you."

Pausing to gather his thoughts, he came up with a plan. They put Brooks back in his pen, and the two of them walked away.

"Do me a favor," Dad said. "Give me five minutes, and then take Brooks out for another walk right here." There was a trailer parked about thirty yards from where they were standing. "I'll be watching from behind that trailer, but you mustn't let him know I'm there."

He hid while Jen walked Brooks back and forth. Sure enough, he started to favor that right side. Dad felt like Mike Tyson had slugged him in the stomach. It seemed that the time had come. The doctor had given him five years, and they were well into six.

When Brooks saw Dad approach, he immediately straightened up and acted as if nothing was wrong. In fact, he ran up to Dad and started to throw kisses his way in an attempt to mask his little performance. Brooks was like a kid caught with his hand in the cookie jar. Even though he pretended to act normally, Brooks knew the jig was up.

Dad continued to work that day, wrestling with the thought that he might never run his boy in agility competition again. He scratched Brooks from the remaining three events they were slated to compete in that weekend.

When he showed up to work the trial the next morning, he sat in the tent and stared at the empty x-pen Brooks had occupied the day before. He picked up the extra lead that was hanging from the open door and held it tight. He fought the urge to well up. *Seven years of doing this—and for what?*

Looking up, he started to talk to himself and perhaps even to God. "We aren't finished here," he shouted. "This isn't done yet. Sure we had our chances, but there's more to do!" Putting the lead in his pocket for good luck, he bowed his head for a moment, turned, and walked away. "Say it ain't so. Please say it ain't so."

Chapter 36
All Things Must Pass

What started out to be a most promising weekend couldn't have turned out worse if someone had scripted it. Great weather, good friends, and acing the jumper's course were all insignificant in comparison to having to scratch the final three events.

The day after the trial, Dad took a rare sick day off from work, his first in nine years. He had gotten an appointment for Brooks at the animal clinic. One advantage to the new clinic was that he could see any of the four veterinarians. All of them knew his dog well and loved seeing him.

Brookie loved going there since he loved being made over.

Dr. Zimbulous saw them that morning. She was an expert on canine joint problems. In fact, before she came to work at the clinic, she had happened to be the one who X-rayed his hips way back when.

Dad trusted her opinion. He explained in detail his concerns about what had happened over the weekend and asked her to do a thorough examination.

Granting Dad's request, the doctor did every test she could muster within the resources of the clinic. After all the prods, stretches, and pokes were complete, they sat and talked.

"Brooks is okay for now," she explained. "He does have some inflammation affecting that right hip, but it's nothing that some medication won't help."

Dad breathed a huge sigh of relief.

She continued, "That doesn't mean he's out of the woods though. He is getting old, and scratching him from the trial was a wise move. The jumping and tight turns when he competes cause the swelling and pain. The more you do as he ages, the more the pain will increase."

Dad drew a deep breath and asked, "So what exactly are you telling me?"

She brought Brooks close to her and started stroking his head. "I'm saying I think you should consider scaling back his agility activities."

"Like how much?"

The doctor gave a deep sigh. "If he was my dog, all the way. But knowing him like I do, that would do him in more than continuing. In your case, I'd do it gradually. Lower the jumps, and keep him from turning hard. He has tremendous drive and will to please. Shutting him down completely—though it would help keep down the swelling—would take away his spirit."

Dad was disheartened; it wasn't what he wanted to hear, but he had a feeling that it was what he was going up against.

Standing to make her exit, she said, "It's up to you, but I know you will make the right decision."

It was hard at first. The rest of the 1999 season was ahead of them, and going to trials with Mom and Sam just wasn't the same without his boy. Well-wishers approached and said how much they missed Brooks. It was nice, but it aggravated the urge to get him out there one last time.

The demo scene was nice, but nothing more. The fast-paced, high-speed duals with Bridget were substituted with demonstrating how certain obstacles should be performed, contacts excluded. Occasionally when Dad thought he was up to it, the weaves were performed to the delight of the crowd. With all that twisting, Brooks had to be careful how often he performed them.

By Christmas that year, Brooks was all but retired. His regular checkups were revealing that the arthritis was setting in fast and hard. Dad didn't know which was worse for Brookie, watching all his pals work out on the equipment in the backyard and not being able to play or the pain in his hips. Those long wish lists to Santa were pared down to one request: *Please let me run again.*

December 29, 1999, was a nice day. Dad decided to do something they hadn't done in years; they went for a walk at Peddler's Village. Brooks seemed up for it, and they had nothing better to do. What the heck? It would be good to get out. In fact, they decided to bring all three dogs.

Dad had Brooks on a long lead and Sam on a short one so they wouldn't get tangled.

Mom guided Vanah, since she was completely blind by then. As they meandered through the town, they came upon a family that was window-shopping in front of a toy store.

When Dad passed by, the little boy turned and said, "Look, Dad. It's Brooks."

Brooks and Dad turned to see who had recognized him.

"It's him," the little boy screamed and ran up to give the dog a big hug.

The father grabbed the child, trying to contain his enthusiasm. "You mustn't go up to strange dogs!"

"No, no," the boy shouted. "He's not a strange dog. I know him." He broke away, ran up to Brooks, and hugged him.

For a brief moment, Dad was nervous that Brooks might not like a stranger running up to him since he had the pain of his hips to contend with, but it all happened so quickly that he had no time to react.

Much to everyone's relief, it was a joyous reunion.

"I'm really sorry about that," the man said. "He really knows better."

"No problem," Dad said. He knelt down next to the boy and asked, "How do you know Brooks?"

Excitedly the boy explained, "I saw him chase a nurse where my Nana lives."

"My god. That was almost two years ago, but I do remember that!"

The boy's mother approached and said, "Oh, he has a great memory when it comes to that day. We all enjoyed the show you guys put on for my mom and the rest of the folks there. It was all they talked about for weeks on end. Brice has seen your dog perform several times since and has pestered us to death to find him a dog like yours."

Dad smiled and said, "I apologize for that. Brooks and I are flattered that he has a fan so young."

"No need to apologize. I have told him when he gets a little older, we'll see," she added.

Mom joined the fray. While the adults talked, Dad noticed that Brooks was enjoying the attention from his newfound friend. His tail was going a mile a minute. When Dad looked down, he saw that divine spark rekindle his spirit and put a smile on the boy's face. Dad turned to Brice and whispered, "Would you like to watch him do a trick just for you?"

"He would do that for me?"

"You hold his lead. Stay right here, and I'll have a surprise for you." Dad handed Sammy's lead to Mom and said, "I'll be right back."

Dad sprinted to the truck, hoping that the set of old weave poles was still stashed under the backseat. He closed his eyes as he opened the back and prayed, "Please, God, let them be there." To his relief, there were nine usable poles, enough for what he wanted them for.

Dad found an area in the grass and stuck the poles in the ground.

Brice was getting excited. He knew what the surprise was that Dad had promised him.

Brooks knew what was up and shook with excitement.

Taking hold of the lead from Brice, Dad led Brooks up to the poles and put him in a sit.

Mom came over to him and whispered, "Are you sure he's okay to do this?"

Dad looked down at Brooks, and the look he gave Dad will always be etched on his mind. The dog's eyes sparkled with life as he reared back his shoulders and said, "I am king of the poles stance."

"He's never been more okay in his life," Dad said as he admired his boy. "Weave, boy, weave!"

Brooks hesitated for a moment. Instead of hitting the poles in his usual form, he charged his dad, jumping up and giving him kisses as he never had before. For that brief moment, his love for Dad eclipsed his worship for the weaves.

Even though the small crowd had no idea what was going on, they cheered loud and hard. When Brookie did perform, it wasn't the Sixers demo, but it might as well have been. He flashed through those poles like they weren't even there. With each pass, the cheers got louder, drawing vendors from their shops to see and cheer one happy, happy dog and his man!

That day was the last time Brooks ever performed the weave poles. Seven weeks later, on February 18, 2000, Champion Jashes Atticus of Ubar—better known as Brooks Robinson Loveless—passed over the Rainbow Bridge.

Brooks left the world on a Friday. The next day, Dad had to chair a training committee meeting. How he got through it without letting on that he had lost his dearest friend the night before was one for the books.

Even when they brought up the idea of a demo that might be tailored to Brooks, he never let on about his loss.

When Sunday rolled around, Dad went to church. Although he wasn't an outwardly religious man, he did try to get to services at every opportunity he could. His habit of getting to trials early carried over to church. Being there first let him enjoy the quiet so he could contemplate his existence in his otherwise unique life.

Sitting alone in the pew, he reflected on his lost friend and how lonely it was going to be without him. Another loss he would suffer was his popular Brooks World article. Writing those little ditties every month or so had given him comfort, especially after his boy retired from competition. No more Christmas lists or writing from the view of life in his dog's perspective. Waiting for the Mass to start inspired a final writing.

I don't consider myself to be a very religious person, although I try to go to church on Sundays whenever I get the chance. Lately, I have been talking to the big guy more and more, hoping that he can convince me that there really is a Rainbow Bridge, and my Brookie is there waiting for me.

Last Sunday, I got to services early so I could get a seat as far away from the choir as possible. While I was meditating on world events, the pastor came over and said he needed to see me after mass. Good grief, *I thought.* He must have noticed that I lip sang "Ave Maria."

Being the good parishioner that I am, I met with him and couldn't believe what he was telling me. He'd had a vision the night before from Saint Francis (patron saint of animals). He wanted to know where the dog they call Brooks had come from. When he got to the Pearly Gates, he thought it was a winged agility jump and leaped over it, landing on cloud nine. He proceeded to herd the sheep out of heaven and caused a massive insomnia epidemic throughout the entire universe. Next, he took his halo to Saint Joseph and made him play Frisbee with it. Saint Peter was so impressed with his performance that he entered a RBDAA (Rainbow Bridge Dog Agility Association) agility trial. Brooks and Pete made quite a pair. They whizzed around the course in record time, clearing jumps like they weren't there. They made him do the weaves twice because no one had seen him do it the first time because he was so fast. There was only one thing wrong. He was so fast that he jumped over all the yellow contacts. When God disqualified him, Saint Peter was so upset that he ordered that there be no yellow in the rainbow. Brooks now qualifies in every run with ease.

I would like to take a moment to thank everyone in our great club for all the support they have given Leslie and me during this difficult time. I have always wanted the club to be a place where we, as members, supported one another in good times as well as bad—and that is just what we have. You all are the greatest, and we couldn't get through this without you. Thanks again, and I hope a new little Terv will soon become a topic in our newsletter.

The topic of the newsletter Dad had promised came true sooner than anyone thought. Fifty-five days after he lost Brooks, he adopted me as his successor. He retired his Brooks World feature for obvious reasons and replaced it with Finley's Planet. Even though there wasn't much to write about since I was new to the scene, the news of my arrival was the happiest article Dad had ever written.

As I explained way back when, I never had the opportunity to meet the great Brooks Loveless, but as you can tell, there was little I didn't know about him. Brooks taught Dad that there was more to life than titles and ribbons, and as you can tell, his spirit lived on long after he passed. Loyalty, the desire to please, and love are what give a dog heart. I may have had big paws, but Brooks was the one who taught me how to have an even bigger heart.